ART AND COOK

LOVE FOOD, LIVE DESIGN AND DREAM ART

ALLAN BEN

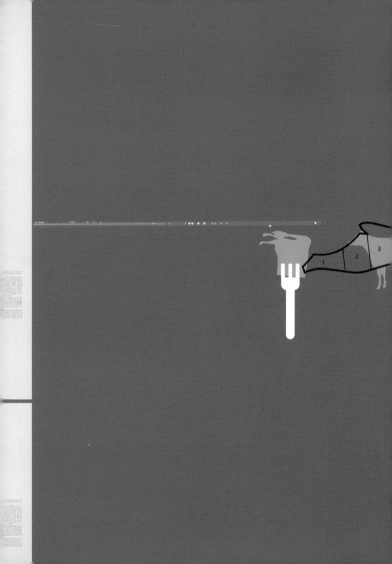

ART AND COOK

LOVE FOOD, LIVE DESIGN AND DREAM ART

AUTHOR: ALLAN BEN

ART AND COOK

LOVE FOOD, LIVE DESIGN AND DREAM ART

ALLAN BEN

Digital In Space Inc.
44-15 14th Avenue
Brooklyn, NY 11219
PHONE (718) 431-9242
FAX (718) 431-9241
info@artandcook.com
www.artandcook.com

Publisher: Allan Ben
Chief Executive Officer: Allan Ben
Photographer: Allan Ben
Photo Assistant: Meytal Toorgeman
Art Director/Graphics Designer: Emmanuel Paletz
Copy Editor/Writer: Lynn Granger
Research and Development: Emmanuel Paletz
Senior Retoucher: Gary Gene Jefferson
Retouchers: Shoshana Kirchenboum, Leslei Malon, Jennifer Even
Production Manager: Shlomy Elkayam
Production Assistant: Mitchell Lincon
Recipe Developer: Einav Gefen Dubnikov
Food Stylists: Liron Meller, Melanie R. Underwood
Coordinator: Molly Gerrasy
Home Economists: Howard Perl, Steve Rozen
Art & Cook was designed and produced by
Allan Ben Studio Inc.
44-15 14th Avenue
Brooklyn, NY 11219
Tel: (718) 431-9244
e-mail: allan@allanben.com

First published in the United States of America in 2005
by Universe Publishing, a division of Rizzoli International Publications, Inc.
300 Park Avenue South
New York, New York 10010
www.rizzoliusa.com
2005 2006 2007 2008 2009 / 10 9 8 7 6 5 4 3 2 1
Printed in China
Library of Congress Control Number: 2005903842
ISBN: 0-7893-1297-2

NOTES

Bracketed terms are intended for American readers.
For all recipes, quantities are given in both metric and imperial measures and, where appropriate, measures are also given
in standard cups and spoons. Follow one set, but not a mixture, because they are not interchangeable.

Standard spoon and cup measures are level.
1 tsp = 5 ml, 1 tbsp = 15 ml, 1 cup = 250 ml/8 fl oz
Australian standard tablespoons are 20 ml. Australian readers should use 3 tsp in place of 1 tbsp for measuring small
quantities of flour, salt, etc.

INTRODUCTION

WE LOVE FOOD, WE LIVE DESIGN AND WE DREAM ART.

"Art & Cook" is a comprehensive volume produced, conceptualized and designed by Allan Ben Studio that blends together Surrealism and Dadaism to create original works of art with universal appeal. The publication also draws from Pop and Commercial Art in its quest to explore bold directions, unconventional ideas and a fresh, new perspective.

The Dada Movement, introduced at the end of the First World War, in opposition to the war, created art that reflected the ugliness of conflict – the anti-art. Other forms of art in the 20th century were impacted by the Dada Movement, among them Surrealism, Abstract Expressionism, Conceptual Art and Pop Art.

While Dadaism is devoid of guidelines and structure (as is the case with the title, used in a manner that is grammatically incorrect to summon forth feelings of shock and consternation), Surrealism draws heavily on theories adapted from Sigmund Freud: It fuses together "conscious and unconscious realms of experience so completely, joining the everyday rational world in an absolute reality, a surreality."

The creative expressions within the confines of this book [that provide a delicate balance between food and art], like Surrealism and Dadaism, are indicative of a desire to draw from reality, fantasy and personal emotions to create images real or imagined – all intended to stimulate the senses and nourish the mind.

The recipes in this volume are influenced by food from the Mediterranean and Asia, Continental American Cuisine and Classic French Cuisine. Food, like art, is a representation of beauty and, when expertly presented, a masterpiece in its own right.

The multifaceted, universal nature of the recipe manifested in the titles, one such being "Grilled Chic Skewers over Grilled Zucchini in Curry and Cr Noodles." What one gets from one taste, one loo universality: a blending together of different flavors spices, in very much the same way an artist mixes cc in search of depth, meaning and tones to evok particular response.

Unparalleled creativity is the hallmark of "Art & Cook the art and recipes in this volume exemplify exploration into uncharted territory in pursuance of extraordinary.

The artwork "Mona Lisa with Moustache," is given a spin by the artist, who, in a paradoxical twist, replaces moustache with two red peppers – the color red conno emotion, in this case, anger.

From the book "Man Ray – Masters of Photogra Series" by Jed Perl, a photo revealing the close-up woman in tears is reassembled. Droplets of water substituted with green lentils in a gesture of symbo (rounded lentils, a metaphor for salty teardrops).

Above all, the images in "Art & Cook," some hauntin their intensity, raise one's level of consciousness ab social, political and moral issues such as world con environmental concerns, animal cruelty and medical technological advances. The visuals tell a story oftentimes, court controversy (see art references).

This book is for those who appreciate all that life ha offer. It's an invitation for the reader to reflect, learn, th laugh and view the world through different lenses.

ALLAN BEN

an Ben has been described by Studio Photography
Design, as "an artist and a businessman, just as
ncerned with creating an effective piece, as he is
h doing his work, in a way that makes objects
otional."

e publication refers to the passion Ben brings to his
rk in his dual role as artist and businessman, since
is the President and CEO of Allan Ben Studio, Inc.,
d involved in running his business with the same
gree of intensity he brings to his photography and
sign.

er graduating from Manhattan's School of Visual Art
h a bachelor's degree in Photography in the early
eties, Ben immediately opened his studio in
nhattan and delved into work in the world of
hion.

Since then he has photographed food and fashion
accessories such as boots, wallets, sunglasses, jewelry,
and is busy at work putting the finishing touches on his
studio's biggest and most prestigious project to date: a
cookbook titled "Art & Cook" that draws the correlation
between food an art in a manner that is creative and
eclectic. The publication blends together Surrealism
and Dadaism to create works of art with universal
appeal.

All that Ben has learned from being an artist and
photographer in New York has prepared him to finally
realize his dream of producing, conceptualizing and
designing "Art & Cook."

"This publication is the realization of a dream come
true for me," says Ben. "In all my years of creating,
exploring and dealing with the competition all around,
I am now involved in a monumental project that is the
sum total of all of my experiences."

"FIRST, YOU EAT WITH YOUR EYES, THEN
YOU LET YOUR SENSES TAKE OVER."

APPETIZERS

BOREKA (FILO PARCEL)
Serves 6-8

13 ounces feta cheese
2 eggs, lightly beaten
1/3 cup chopped fresh parsley
12 ounces filo pastry
1/3 cup good quality olive oil
Freshly ground black pepper

Preheat oven to 350 degrees F.

■ Lightly grease a baking sheet. Crumble the feta cheese into a large bowl using a fork or your fingers. Mix in the eggs and parsley and season with freshly ground black pepper.

■ Cover the filo pastry with a damp towel to prevent it from drying out. Remove one sheet at a time. Brush each sheet lightly with olive oil and layer 4 sheets on top of one another. Cut the pastry into four even strips.

■ Place 2 rounded teaspoons of the feta mixture in one corner of each strip and fold diagonally, creating a triangular pillow. Place on the baking sheet, seam-side down, and brush with olive oil. Repeat with the remaining pastry and filling to make 24 parcels. Bake for 20 minutes, or until golden on the top as well as the bottom.

■ Serve warm as a light appetizer or as part of a large meze plate.

■ Note: Fillings for borekas are versatile and can be adapted to include your favorite cheeses such as Haloumi, Gruyere, Cheddar or Mozzarella.

GRILLED PORTOBELLO MUSHROOM WITH ARUGULA SALAD

Serves 4

4 Portobello mushrooms (1 per person)
2 tablespoons fresh thyme leaves
1/3 cup Olive oil
1 bunch arugula
3 tablespoons extra virgin olive oil
1 tablespoons lemon juice
Salt and pepper

■ Heat a griddle or a grilling pan. Brush portobellos with olive oil, season with salt and pepper and sprinkle with fresh thyme leaves.
Place in the pan top side down for 1 minute, turn mushrooms 90 degrees to make criss-cross marks.

■ Flip sides and cook for 2 more minutes. Set aside.

■ Wash and dry the arugula. Toss with the extra virgin olive oil, salt, pepper and lemon juice.

■ Cut the mushrooms on the bias. Place a small amount of the seasoned arugula at the side of the plate and fan the mushroom next to it.

EGGPLANT AND LAMB PACKAGES WITH SUN-DRIED TOMATO VINAIGRETTE AND BABY SPINACH

Serves 4

3 ounces margarine, cut into small dices and chilled
1 cup flour
1/4 cup ice cold water
Salt and pepper
2 medium eggplants
1/2 cup olive oil
8 ounces ground lamb meat
2 shallots, chopped
2 garlic cloves, minced
1/3 cup fresh basil leaves, julienne
1/4 cup sun-dried tomatoes in oil, strained
3 tablespoons sherry wine vinegar
2/3 cup extra virgin olive oil
1 garlic clove
2 cups baby spinach, washed and dried
2 tablespoons lemon juice
2 tablespoons extra virgin olive oil
1 egg, beaten
Salt & pepper

Preheat oven to 350 degrees F.

■ In a food processor combine the flour with the salt. Add the butter and work to a grainy texture. Add the water and work for 5 seconds. Transfer the dough to a floured surface and knead quickly to a smooth soft (but not sticky) dough. Form a disk and place in the fridge for 20 minutes.

■ Cut the eggplants to 1/2 inch thick circles, brush with oil on both sides and place on a baking sheet. Bake for 15-20 minutes until almost fully cooked. Let cool.

■ In a blender puree the sun dried tomato and the garlic. Add the vinegar and blend to combine. While blending add the extra virgin olive oil slowly and season with salt and pepper.

■ Roll the dough on a floured surface to 1/8-inch thick and cut out four 6-inch diameter circles. Mix the lamb meat, shallots, garlic and basil and season well with salt and pepper. Place 1 tablespoon of the meat mixture between two slices of eggplant and place the sandwich at the center of the dough circle. Wrap the eggplant with the dough making sure it is sealed and place it on a baking sheet with the smooth side up. Repeat with the rest of the slices.

■ Brush the top with the beaten egg and bake for 20 minutes until golden.

■ Mix the baby spinach with the lemon juice and olive oil, season with salt and place in the center of a serving plate. Top with the eggplant and lamb package and drizzle around with vinaigrette. Serve warm.

STUFFED GRAPE LEAVES
Serves 6-8

ounce packet vine leaves in brine
up medium-grain rice
mall onion, finely chopped
blespoon olive oil
unces pine nuts, toasted
blespoons currants

2 tablespoons chopped fresh dill
1 tablespoon finely chopped fresh mint
1 tablespoon finely chopped fresh flat-leaf parsley
1/3 cup extra virgin olive oil
2 tablespoons lemon juice
2 cups vegetable stock

Soak the leaves in cold water for 15 minutes, then
ove and pat dry. Cut off any stems. Reserve some
es to line the saucepan and discard any that have
es or look poor. Meanwhile, soak the rice in boiling
er for 10 minutes to soften, then drain.

Place the rice, onion, olive oil, pine nuts, currants,
os and salt and pepper in a large bowl and mix well.

Lay some leaves vein side down on a flat surface.
e 1 tablespoon of filling in the center of each, fold
stalk end over the filling, then the left and right sides
 the center, and finally roll firmly towards the tip to
emble a small cigar. Repeat with the remaining filling
leaves.

■ Use the reserved vine leaves to line the base of a
large heavy-based saucepan. Drizzle with 1 tablespoon
olive oil. Add the stuffed leaves, packing them tightly in
one layer, then pour the remaining oil and the lemon
juice over them.

■ Pour the stock over and cover with an inverted plate
to prevent the stuffed vine leaves from moving around
while cooking. Bring to a boil, and then reduce to a
simmer, covered, for 45 minutes. Remove with a slotted
spoon. Serve warm or cold with lemon wedges.

TOMATO PATTIES WITH YOGURT SAUC
Serves 6

■ Sauté the onion in the olive oil for 2-3 minutes, until translucent. Add the garlic and sauté for an additional minute. Drain.

■ Mix the fresh tomatoes, sun dried tomatoes, parsley, mint and oregano. In a separate bowl sift the flour and the baking powder and add that to the "wet" ingredients. Combine well to achieve a thick batter. Add flour if necessary and season well with salt and pepper. Mix in the sautéed onion and garlic and let rest in the refriger for at least one hour.

Preparation - Yogurt Sauce:
■ Peel the cucumber and grate finely. Mix the cucum garlic, mint and yogurt and season with salt and peppe taste. Keep in the refrigerator until ready to be used. M small patties and deep-fry in oil heated 375 degree Serve with yogurt sauce.

1/2 cups peeled, seeded and
[di]ced tomatoes (about 4-5
[to]matoes)
[...] cup finely chopped sundried
[to]matoes
[...]up chopped parsley
[...] cup chopped scallions, green
[pa]rt only

1/2 cup chopped mint leaves
1 teaspoon dried oregano
1 1/2 cups flour
1 tablespoon baking powder
3/4 cup chopped onion
2 cloves garlic, minced
2 tablespoons olive oil
vegetable oil for deep-frying

2 cups whole milk yogurt
1 clove garlic, minced
1 cucumber
2 tablespoons chopped mint
leaves
Salt and black pepper

"FOOD, LIKE ART, STIMULATES THE MIND
AND THE SENSES."

SOUPS

Serves 4-6

4 large Idaho potatoes, peeled and diced
2 leeks, white part only, washed and sliced
1 small onion, chopped
1/4 cup chopped celery
2 ounces butter
3 cups water
1 1/2 cups skim milk
1/2 teaspoon salt
1/8 teaspoon pepper

■ Heat the butter in a pot until melted and translucent. Sauté the onions, leeks and celery for 5 minutes stirring occasionally. Add the potatoes and season well with salt and pepper.

■ Add the water and milk and bring to a boil; reduce to low heat, cover and cook for 45 minutes or until pota and leeks are very soft.

■ Transfer carefully to a processor and puree for minutes to a chunky texture (p to a smooth texture if desired)

■ Serve the soup with "matches" or young ce leaves.

FRENCH ONION SOUP
Serves 4-6

4 tablespoons butter or margarine
10 cups sliced Spanish onions
2 cloves garlic, minced
2 tablespoons Tamari soy sauce
1 tablespoon dark brown sugar
2 cups white wine
11/2 quarts vegetable stock or water

1 1/2 teaspoons fresh thyme leaves
1 stem rosemary
1 egg, beaten
Salt and pepper
1 package puff pastry
1/2 cup grated Parmesan cheese (optional)
Ovenproof soup bowls

eat oven to 400 degrees F.

Melt butter in a 4-quart pot and sauté onions and
c until soft and golden, but not brown. Add the soy
ce and sugar and let cook for 5 additional minutes.
the white wine, bring to a boil and let cook until
ced by half; add the stock, herbs and season well
salt and pepper. Bring to a boil, reduce flame and
immer for 40 minutes. Let cool before preparing to
e.

Cut disks out of the dough, big enough to cover the
of the soup plates well, then cut out a small circle
he middle of each disk. Ladle the soup into the

ovenproof bowls and brush the rims with the beaten
egg, placing the puff pastry disks immediately on top.
Pinch with your fingers to make sure the dough is
"glued" to the dish. Brush the dough lightly with the
remainder of the egg and sprinkle with the cheese.
Place in the oven and bake for 15-20 minutes until the
dough is golden and baked all around. Serve
immediately.

■ The soup can be served without the puff pastry
"cover" or the disks can be baked separately and
served with the soup. Serve hot.

CARROT AND GINGER SOUP
Serves 4-6

7 medium size carrots
2 tablespoons peeled and grated
fresh ginger
2 tablespoons oil
Sea salt
White pepper
2 cans coconut milk
5-6 cups vegetable stock
1/4 cup cilantro leaves
Whole milk yogurt for serving
Mint leaves for garnish

■ Peel and slice carrots (1/8-inch thick). Heat the oil in a big pot until hot but not smoking. Add the carrots and sauté for 3-4 minutes. Add the ginger and coconut milk, cook for 4 minutes, then include 5 cups vegetable stock. Season with salt and pepper and reduce to medium low heat. Cook for 40 minutes or until carrots are very soft. Puree soup to a smooth texture with an emulsifying blender or in a food processor with the metal bla... soup is too thick add some of the remaining stock... pouring until the desired texture is achieved. Ad... cilantro and puree for one minute more. Chec... seasoning and add salt and pepper if needed.

■ Pour into serving plates, place a spoonful of yog... the middle of the plates and garnish with mint leave...

CHICKEN MISO SOUP WITH MATZO BALL DUMPLINGS

Serves 4

4 large eggs
1 teaspoon salt
1/2 cup fennel, finely diced
2 tablespoons fresh dill
1 tablespoon chopped chives
2 tablespoons chopped fresh parsley
1/3 cup plus 1 tablespoon seltzer
1 cup matzo meal
Dash ground black pepper
1 to 2 teaspoons finely chopped peeled fresh ginger
6 cups chicken stock
2 tablespoons miso paste
1/4 cup basil leaves, julienne

■ Beat eggs and 1 teaspoon salt for 1 minute. Stir in fennel, dill, and chives or parsley, followed by the seltzer. Fold in matzo meal, pepper, and ginger until well blended. Cover and refrigerate for 1 to 4 hours.

■ Wet hands, and form the matzo balls. Drop the balls into a large pot of boiling salted water; cover, reduce heat, and simmer for 30 minutes. When the matzo balls are almost cooked, heat chicken stock in a soup pot. Add the miso paste and taste. If needed, season with salt and pepper.

■ When matzo balls are finished, add them to the stock.

■ Ladle the stock into warmed bowls and add 2 matzo balls to each serving. Sprinkle with the basil julienne and serve.

EGG DROP BEEF SOUP WITH RAMEN NOODLES
Serves 4-6

12 ounces beef (boneless sirloin or flank steak)
2 teaspoons cornstarch
1/2 teaspoon salt
Dash white pepper
3 tablespoons cornstarch
3 tablespoons water
3 eggs
1/2 teaspoon salt

6 cups good quality beef broth
4 thin slices peeled fresh gingerroot
2 tablespoons Tamari soy sauce
1/2 cup chopped scallion
1 package Ramen noodles, cooked

Trim fat from beefsteak; cut beef lengthwise into 2-
[i]n strips. Cut strips crosswise into 1/8-inch slices.
[i]s beef, 1/2 teaspoon cornstarch, 1/4 teaspoon salt
[ ] the white pepper in medium bowl. Cover and
[re]igerate for 20 minutes. Mix 2 tablespoons
[co]rnstarch and water. Beat eggs and 1/2 teaspoon

[H]eat broth to boiling in a 3-quart saucepan. Add
[g]ingerroot and soy sauce, bring to a boil and let boil

for 2 minutes. Add beef; stir to separate the pieces.
Heat to boiling, stirring constantly. Stir in cornstarch
mixture and whisk well until the soup is boiling again
then drizzle the egg mixture slowly into broth, stirring
constantly with fork, until eggs form threads. Remove
gingerroot.

■ Place a handful of the noodles in a serving bowl,
ladle soup on top, sprinkle with scallion and serve.

GRILLED CHICKEN SOUP WITH CARROT DUMPLINGS

Serves 6-8

2 pounds chicken bones
1 big onion quartered, skin on
2 carrots, roughly sliced
3 celery stalks, roughly sliced
2 parsnips, roughly sliced
2 tablespoons olive oil
1 bay leaf
5 stems parsley
1 stem thyme
Salt and pepper
2 pounds chicken breast, boned and cleaned
3 tablespoons olive oil
1 tablespoon thyme leaves
2 garlic cloves, minced
2 medium carrots, peeled and cut to 1/2 inch pieces
1 medium Idaho potato, peeled and cut to 1/2 inch pieces
1 whole egg
5-6 tablespoons flour

Preheat oven to 400 degrees F.

▦ Spread the chicken bones on a baking sheet and place in the oven. Roast for 30 minutes until the bones are golden brown.

▦ In a soup pot, sauté the onion, carrot slices, celery and parsnips in the olive oil for 3 minutes. Add the chicken bones scraping the tray well; add 2 quarts water and season with salt and pepper. When the soup comes to a boil, skim the top, reduce to a simmer, add the bay leaf, thyme and parsley and let simmer for 11/2 hours.

▦ Strain the soup and taste, season as needed.

▦ While the soup is cooking prepare the dumplings, place the carrot and potato chunks in a small pot, cover with water and season with salt. Cook for about 20 minutes until very soft but not falling apart. Strain and let stand for 10 minutes to cool. When cool puree to a smooth

texture with a hand blender or food processor. Transfer to a metal bowl and mix in the egg. Mix in flour 2 spoons at a time until it but sticky, season with salt pepper. Bring a pot with water boil and season with salt.

▦ Using two teaspoons teaspoon size dumplings into boiling water and cook for 1 min Place the cooked dumplings in cold water to stop the coo process and transfer to a plate.

▦ Rub the chicken breast in oil, garlic and the thyme lea Season well with salt and pe and grill on grill pan or griddle f 5 minutes on each side until cooked. Let cool for 5 minutes then slice 1/8-inch thick, on the using a sharp knife.

▦ Place 5 dumplings in a se plate, along with a few slices o grilled chicken breast and ladle soup on top. Serve immediately

MEAT AND VEGETABLE SOUP
Serves 6

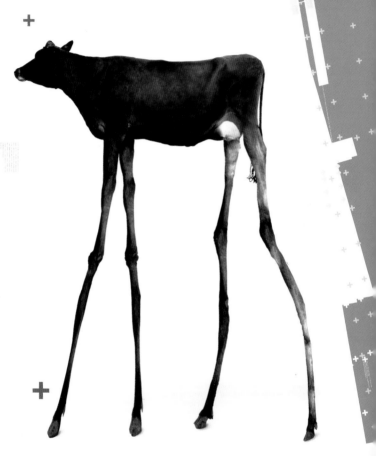

1/3 cup olive oil
1 pound stew meat, cubed (1/2-inch)
2 quarts beef/chicken stock
Salt and pepper
1/3 cup barley
2 onions, thinly sliced
2 cloves garlic, minced
2 stalks celery, diced
1 leek, thinly sliced
1 carrot, cut in half lengthwise and thinly sliced
1 bay leaf
1 large sprig of fresh thyme
12 ounces pumpkin, peeled and cut into small dices
2 medium potatoes cut into small dices
1/2 cup fresh or frozen lima beans or fava beans
1/2 cup fresh or frozen green peas
2 small zucchinis, cut in half lengthwise and thinly sliced
2 ripe tomatoes, peeled and roughly chopped
2 pounds marrow bones
1 cup chopped fresh string beans
16-ounce can tomato puree
2 tablespoons chopped fresh parsley
6 toast points
Sea salt

Preheat oven to 400 degrees F.

■ Place the bones on a baking sheet and bake for about 25-30 minutes until dark brown. Season diced meat with salt and pepper. Heat the oil in a big pot and sauté the seasoned meat for 3 minutes, mixing occasionally, until meat is golden on all sides. Remove the meat and sauté the onion, garlic, celery and leeks for 2 minutes; add the meat, stock, barley, bay leaf, thyme and bones and season well with salt and pepper. Bring to a boil and remove the foam that emerges to the top. Lower flame and simmer covered for 1 1/2 hours.

■ Add the rest of the vegetables, tomato puree, and parsley. Cook for an additional 40 minutes.

■ Remove the bones and use a small knife to remove the bone marrow. Spread the bone marrow on the toast points and sprinkle with the sea salt. Ladle the soup into serving bowls and serve hot with a toast point.

"CREATING A DISH IS LIKE TOURING THE WORLD, TAKING DIFFERENT FLAVORS AND TEXTURES FROM EACH CONTINENT TO CREATE A SYMBOL OF PERFECTION."

SALADS

COLORFUL NICOISE SALAD WITH GRILLED FRESH TUNA
Serves 4-6

Preparation - Vinaigrette:
Whisk the lemon juice, chopped shallot, garlic and mustard in a mixing bowl. While whisking, add the oil slowly to create emulsification. Season with salt and pepper and check the flavors. If the vinaigrette is too tart add a little more oil; if too "oily" add more lemon juice and mustard.

Preparation - Salad:
■ Cook the haricot vert in salted, boiling water for 2 minutes and remove to ice water to stop the cooking process.

■ Cook the potatoes in, salted water until soft but not falling apart (check with a fork). Drain, cool and cut into quarters.

■ Cut the cherry tomatoes in halves and the hard-boiled eggs into quarters.

■ Warm the oil in a small high saucepan to 350 deg F and carefully add the capers. If the capers are still splashing will occur.
Transfer to a plate lined with paper towel to get ri excess oil.

■ Bring a grilling pan or a griddle to high heat (a s pan or a non-stick pan can also be used). Brush the steaks with the olive oil, season with salt and pepper sprinkle with the thyme leaves. Place the steaks grilling pan and grill each side for one minute. Rem from the heat.

■ Mix the greens, tomatoes, beans, green beans, b potatoes and anchovy; toss with the vinaigrette and p the eggs and the tuna randomly on the salad. Drizzle vinaigrette and serve.

the Dressing:
cup lemon juice
blespoon chopped shallot
all garlic clove minced
aspoon Dijon mustard
p extra virgin olive oil
and black pepper

the Salad:
und mixed salad greens
p basil leaves (not packed)
d onion, thinly sliced
edium purple potatoes or new potatoes
pound cherry tomatoes (yellow, orange, red)
pound haricot vert (French green beans)
p kidney beans, drained
nces Nicoise olives, pitted
e-ounce tuna steaks
blespoons olive oil for tuna
blespoon fresh thyme leaves
and pepper
rd-boiled eggs
p capers, drained and dried
ps vegetable oil

HUMMUS – MEDITERRANEAN CHICK-PEA PASTE

Serves 4-6

■ Place the chickpeas in a bowl, add 1 quart water, and soak overnight. Drain and place in a large saucepan with 2 quarts water (or enough to cover the chickpeas by 2 inches), bay leaf, onion and a carrot. Bring to boil, then reduce to a simmer for 1 hour 15 minutes, or until the chickpeas are very tender. Skim surface.

■ Discard the onion, carrot and bay leaf. Drain well reserving the cooking liquid and leave until cool enough to handle. Pick through for any loose skins and discard.

■ Blend the chickpeas, tahini, garlic, cu[...] lemon juice, olive oil, cayenne pepper and [...] teaspoon salt in a food processor until thick [...] smooth. With the motor running, gradually [...] enough of the reserved cooking liquid, about [...] cup, to form a smooth creamy purée. Season w[...] salt and lemon juice. Spread onto flat bowls [...] plates, drizzle with extra virgin olive oil, spri[...] with paprika and scatter parsley over the [...] Serve with warm pita bread.

1 carrot, quartered
1 cup dried chickpeas
1 bay leaf
1 onion, quartered
2 tablespoons tahini
4 cloves garlic, crushed
2 teaspoons ground cumin
1/3 cup lemon juice
3 tablespoons olive oil
Large pinch of cayenne pepper
Extra virgin olive oil, to garnish
Paprika, to garnish
Chopped fresh flat-leaf parsley, to garnish

MIDDLE EASTERN CHOPPED SALAD
Serves 4-6

4 large tomatoes
2 cucumbers
1 red or green pepper
1 scallion
2 cloves garlic, minced
1 tablespoon minced fresh parsley
Salt and freshly ground black pepper
3 tablespoons olive oil
3 tablespoons lemon juice
1 teaspoon Za'atar (optional)

Wash tomatoes and dice small. Peel cucumbers and dice. Dice pepper. Finely chop scallions. Place all vegetables in a salad bowl, add remaining ingredients and mix well. Refrigerate until ready to serve. Before serving toss with Za'atar and serve with a crusty bread.

CARROT, PEARL BARLEY AND LIMA BEAN SALAD
Serves 4

1 pound carrots, peeled and diced small
1 cup pearl barley
3 cups vegetable stock
1 tablespoon vegetable oil
1 cup lima beans
2 tablespoons olive oil
1 clove garlic, chopped
1 teaspoon ground cumin
1/4 cup lime juice
2 scallions, green part only, finely sliced
3 tablespoons finely chopped cilantro
Salt and pepper

■ Sauté the barley in the vegetable oil for 30 seconds; add the vegetable stock and season with salt and pepper. Bring to a boil and reduce to a simmer. Let barley cook until tender (about 15 minutes).

■ When done, drain the excess liquids and let cool. Cook the lima beans in salted boiling water for 2 minutes, transfer to ice cold water to stop the cooking and drain.

■ Heat the olive oil in a wide sauté pan and add the garlic and ground cumin. Sauté for 10 seconds and add the diced carrots. Season well with salt and pepper and sauté for 3 additional minutes. Remove from the heat.

■ Combine the carrots (with the oil), barley and lima beans in a big mixing bowl. Toss with the lime juice and mix in the cilantro and scallions. Check for flavor and season accordingly. Serve at room temperature.

GRILLED ENDIVE & ARUGULA SALAD WITH HONEY-TOASTED WALNUTS IN HORSERADISH VINAIGRETTE

Serves 4-6

4 endives, cut to quarters, lengthwise
(and/or radicchio)
3 bunches (handfuls) arugula, washed and
dried
1/2 cup very good extra virgin olive oil
Salt and black pepper
1/4 cup brown sugar
Shredded carrots for garnish

For Honey-toasted Walnuts:
2 cups walnuts
2/3 cup honey
1 tablespoon onion powder
1 teaspoon garlic powder
2 pinches salt
2 pinches cayenne pepper

For the Horseradish Vinaigrette:
(makes 1 1/2 cups of dressing)
1 shallot, chopped
2 tablespoons white horseradish
1 tablespoon sour cream (or mayo)
1-2 tablespoons applesauce
Salt and black pepper
1/3 cup cider vinegar
1 cup olive oil

Preparation – Nuts:
Preheat oven to 300 degrees F.
■ Mix all ingredients together in a mixing bowl, transfer to a baking sheet and toast for 15 minutes (rotating the baking sheet) or until walnuts are almost dark brown. Let cool completely before using.

■ Heat a grilling pan or griddle. Rub the endive quarters with olive oil and season with salt and pepper. Sprinkle with brown sugar and grill all sides until the endives are tender (endives can be "marked" by the grill and placed in a preheated oven for 5 minutes to finish the cooking).

Preparation – Vinaigrette:
■ Mix shallots, horseradish, salt, pepper and sour cr[...] Add the vinegar and mix well. Drizzle the oil slowly [...] mixing to a smooth thick texture. (Can be done [...] emulsifier blender or in a food processor.)

■ Toss the arugula and honey roasted nuts with 1/2 [...] of the vinaigrette in a mixing bowl (add more if nee[...] In another mixing bowl toss the grilled endive with 1/4 [...] of vinaigrette.

■ Pile the arugula nicely on a plate, lean endives o[...] arugula around the plate. Sprinkle with shredded ca[...]

GREEN AND RED LEAVES SALAD WITH DRIED CRANBERRIES, PINEAPPLE-MANGO AND VODKA VINAIGRETTE

Serves 4-6

2 heads frisee lettuce
2 cups red oak leaves or beet greens
1/2 cup dried cranberries
3 ounces Roquefort cheese or Gorgonzola, crumbled (optional)

For the Vinaigrette:
1 cup diced ripe mango
1/2 cup crushed pineapple
1/3 cup vodka (can be flavored)
3 tablespoons sour cream
2 tablespoons white wine vinegar
1/2 -2/3 cup grape seed oil
1 teaspoon honey
Salt and pepper

■ Wash the lettuce and red leaves in cold water and dry well in a lettuce spinner. Place in a big bowl and toss with the cranberries and cheese.

Preparation - Vinaigrette:
■ Place the mango and crushed pineapple in a food processor and puree for 30 seconds. Add the sour cream, vodka and vinegar and puree well. While working, drizzle the oil to create emulsification. Add the honey and season well with salt and pepper.

■ Drizzle some of the vinaigrette over the salad and toss. Check for flavor and seasoning.

TOMATO SALAD WITH WARM GOAT CHEESE, SHAVED RED ONIONS IN WARM BALSAMIC VINAIGRETTE

Serves 4

1 red beefsteak tomato
2 cherry tomatoes
2 yellow tomatoes
1 orange tomato
8-ounce log of fresh goat cheese (like chevre) cut into 8 one-ounce round pieces
8 thin slices of baguette (French bread)
1/3 cup basil leaves, washed and dried

2 tablespoons olive oil
Sea salt
1 shallot, finely diced
1/2 cup good balsamic vinegar
1 teaspoon Dijon mustard
1 cup extra virgin olive oil
Salt and pepper

eat oven to 350 degrees F.
Brush the baguette slices with the olive oil and
e one piece of goat cheese on top. Transfer to a
ng sheet and place in the oven for 4 minutes.

Wash the tomatoes and slice thinly. Julienne basil.
nge the tomatoes on serving plates, alternating
colors, and sprinkle with the sea salt. Top with two
t cheese toasts and sprinkle with the basil strips.

■ Heat 1 tablespoon of the extra virgin olive oil in a
saucepot and sauté the shallots for 2 minutes. Add
the balsamic vinegar and the mustard and whisk
vigorously for 1 minute. Turn off the heat and add the
rest of the oil slowly while whisking. Season with salt
and pepper and drizzle over the tomato salad. Serve
immediately.

"COOKING IS A WAY TO EXPRESS YOURSELF.
A RECIPE IS JUST THE TOOL YOU USE TO DO IT WELL."

PASTA

PENNE WITH LEMON AND POPPY SEED SAUCE

1 pound penne
2 tablespoons unsalted butter at room temperature
2 shallots, finely diced
1 cup light cream
1/2 cup poppy seeds
1/3 cup freshly squeezed lemon juice
1 tablespoon lemon zest
3 tablespoons fresh Italian parsley, chopped
1/4 cup freshly grated or shaved Parmesan cheese

Cook the penne in a large pot of boiling water until al
te (about 8 minutes) and drain.

Grind the poppy seeds in a spice grinder for 10 seconds.
: the butter in a skillet large enough to hold the cooked
a, and sauté the shallots and poppy seeds for 1 minute.
 the cream and lemon zest and bring to a boil, reduce to
mer and let cook for 10 minutes over a low heat.

■ When sauce thickens, add lemon juice and season
with salt and pepper. Add the cooked pasta to the skillet,
away from the heat and toss to blend.

■ Let stand covered for about 2 minutes allowing the
pasta to absorb the sauce. Serve with a sprinkle of fresh
parsley and shaved cheese.

GEMELLI WITH ARTICHOKE HEARTS, KIDNEY BEANS AND TARRAGON

Serves 4

1 package gemelli pasta
8 ounces artichoke hearts, frozen and thawed
2 cups cooked kidney beans, drained
2 garlic cloves, sliced
4 stems fresh tarragon + 1/4 cup fresh tarragon leaves
1 teaspoon fennel seeds
1 cup olive oil
6 ounces smoked turkey breast, diced
Salt and pepper

Heat the oil with the tarragon stems and the
[fen]nel seeds in a small pot for 3 minutes. Turn off
[the] heat and let stand so that the oil will be infused
[with] the tarragon flavor until ready to be used. For
[bett]er results do this a day or two in advance.

[I]n a pot with boiling salted water, cook the
[arti]choke hearts for 2 minutes; remove from the
[wat]er to a bowl with ice-cold water to stop the
[coo]king. Cook the pasta in the same pot until al
[den]te (about 8-10 minutes) and drain.

■ Strain the infused oil and heat 1/3 of a cup in a wide
sauté pan. Add the garlic and sauté for 30 seconds then
add the artichoke hearts and the diced turkey breast and
sauté for 2 more minutes. Add the beans and season well
with salt and pepper. Add the pasta and cook while
stirring occasionally for 1-2 minutes; toss with the
tarragon leaves.

■ Apportion the pasta to serving plates and drizzle with
a little of the remaining oil.

SPAGHETTI WITH ROASTED CHERRY TOMATOES, FENNEL AND SAFFRON SAUCE

Serves 4

1 package Spaghetti
2 pints cherry tomatoes (can be different colors)
1/2 cup extra virgin olive oil
2 stems fresh thyme
1 stem fresh rosemary
1 fennel bulb, diced (keep the fennel leaves for garnish)

2 garlic cloves, minced
3 tablespoons olive oil or butter
2 cups dry white wine
1/3 teaspoon high quality saffron threads
Salt and pepper
1/3 cup grated Parmesan cheese (optional)

heat oven to 375 degrees F.

Toss the cherry tomatoes in a mixing bowl with the ⸻a virgin olive oil, thyme and rosemary stems and ⸻son well with salt and pepper. Spread the tomatoes ⸻a baking sheet and roast in the oven for 10-15 ⸻utes, mixing once, until the tomatoes are lightly ⸻wn. Remove from the oven and let cool.

Cook the pasta in a pot with boiling salted water ⸻l al dente (about 8-10 minutes) and drain.

■ Heat the olive oil in a large sauté pan, add the garlic and diced fennel and cook for 4 minutes. Add the saffron and wine and bring to a boil, allowing the liquid to reduce by half. Season well with salt and pepper. Add the pasta and the roasted tomatoes and cook until thoroughly warm (about 2 minutes).

■ Apportion pasta to serving plates, sprinkle the cheese, garnish with the fennel leaves and serve warm.

GOAT CHEESE RAVIOLI WITH ZUCCHINI AND TOMATO SAUCE

Serves 4

2 1/2 cups unbleached all purpose flour
1 egg + 2 extra large egg yolks
2 tablespoons extra virgin olive oil
1/4 cup cold water
1/2 teaspoon salt
8 ounces soft goat cheese
2 ounces Pecorino Romano cheese, grated
1 garlic clove, minced
1 egg + 1 egg, beaten, for sealing ravioli
2 small zucchini, sliced 1/4-inch thick

1 small onion, cut into thin wedges
1 (14 1/2 ounce) can diced tomatoes
2 tablespoons olive oil
1/2 teaspoon thyme leaves
1 teaspoon chopped fresh tarragon
1 tablespoon chopped fresh basil
2 tablespoons black olives, pitted and sliced
2 tablespoons shredded fresh Parmesan cheese
Salt and pepper

...ace the flour on a working surface and create a ...n the center. Beat the yolks and the egg; add in the ... salt and oil and place in the center. Use a fork to ... incorporating the flour into the egg mixture, ...g small amounts at a time. When the dough is ...enough start working with your hands until you get ...ooth elastic finish. Clean the working area, lightly ...t, then roll the dough (use a pasta machine if one ...ailable) into a thin sheet. Combine the cheeses, ... and egg in a mixing bowl.

...oll the pasta sheet over a ravioli pan or cut out ... shapes using a cutter if ravioli pan is not available. ... a teaspoon of the filling in the center of half of the ...; brush the beaten egg around the edges and top

with the empty cut out ravioli tightening the ravioli well with your thumb and index finger.

■ Bring a pot with salted water to a boil and cook ravioli for 2 minutes. Drain, cover and keep warm.

■ Heat the oil in a wide sauté pan over medium-high heat. Add zucchini and onion; cook and stir 3 to 4 minutes or until vegetables are crisp and tender.

■ Add tomatoes, herbs and olives and cook and stir for 5 minutes. Add cooked ravioli and stir gently.

■ Apportion raviolis to serving plates, sprinkle with the Parmesan cheese and serve.

PENNE WITH CREAM OF ROASTED RE[D] PEPPERS AND GORGONZOLA CHEESE

Serves 4

1 package penne pasta
5 red peppers
3 tablespoons olive oil
2 shallots
2 cloves garlic
1/3 cup sherry wine vinegar

1 cup olive oil
1/3 cup heavy cream
Salt and pepper
8 ounces good Gorgonzola cheese, crumbled
Basil for garnish

Preheat oven to 400 degrees F.

■ Brush the peppers with the oli[ve] and place on a baking sheet. Roas[t] peppers in the oven for about 30 mi[n], turning them often until all side[s] slightly burnt. Remove from the ove[n] big bowl and wrap well with saran

he peppers "sweat" and cool for about 10 minutes using your hands, peel them (the skin should come asily) and discard the tips and the seeds. Place the ed peppers in a blender along with the garlic, shallots ar and oil and puree to a smooth texture. Season well salt and pepper.

ook the pasta in a pot of boiling salted water until al e (about 8-10 minutes), drain.

■ Transfer the red pepper sauce to a wide pan and heat over a medium flame. Add in the cream and mix until well combined. Taste and correct seasoning accordingly. Add the pasta and toss so that the it will be well coated in the sauce. Remove from the heat and mix in the Gorgonzola cheese.

■ Apportion to serving plates, garnish with the basil leaves and serve.

FETTUCCINE WITH LEEKS AND VERMOUTH CREAM SAUCE

Serves 4

1 pound good quality fettuccine
5 leeks, white part only
1-2 ounces butter
2/3 cup dry vermouth
1 tablespoon grainy mustard
Salt and pepper
3 garlic cloves, minced
2 cups heavy cream
1/4 cup thinly sliced basil leaves
Grated Parmesan cheese for serving

■ Bring a big pot (or a pasta pot) with water to a boil and salt the water well. Cook the pasta for 10 minutes or until al dente. Drain the pasta and set aside one cup of the cooking water.

■ Melt the butter in a big sauté pan, add the leeks and garlic and stir. Let cook over a medium heat for about 5 minutes until leeks start to soften and turn golden. Add the vermouth and reduce to low-medium heat, cook for 2 minutes, then add the cream and mustard. Season with salt and pepper and cook for 5-10 minutes or until the cream thickens. If the sauce is too thick add a little of the pasta cooking liquid.

■ Add the fettuccini and cook it in the sauce for 2 minutes. Add the sliced basil leaves and transfer to a serving platter. Sprinkle with grated Parmesan cheese.

SPAGHETTI PUTTANESCA
Serves 4

1 package spaghetti
1/3 cup olive oil
2 onions, finely chopped
3 cloves garlic, finely chopped
1/2 teaspoon chili flakes
6 large ripe tomatoes, diced
4 tablespoons capers, rinsed
8 anchovies in oil, drained, chopped
5 ounces Kalamata olives, pitted
3 tablespoons chopped fresh flat-leaf parsley

■ Heat oil in a saucepan, add the onion and cook over medium heat for 5 minutes. Add the garlic and chili flakes to the saucepan and cook for 30 seconds. Add the tomato, capers and anchovies. Simmer over low heat for 10-15 minutes, or until the sauce is thick and pulpy. Stir in the olives and the parsley.

■ While the sauce is cooking, cook the spaghetti in a large pot of boiling salted water until al dente. Drain and return to the pan.

■ Add the sauce to the pasta and stir through. Season with salt and freshly ground black pepper, to taste, and serve immediately.

FETTUCCINE ALFREDO WITH ASPARAGUS TIPS AND WALNUT OIL

Serves 4

8 ounces dried spinach fettuccine
4 tablespoons butter
1 garlic clove, minced
2/3 cup heavy cream
1 cup grated Parmesan cheese
1 bunch asparagus
1 tablespoon walnut oil
Cracked black pepper
2/3 cup roasted walnuts
Salt

■ Cut the top inch (tips) of the asparagus and cook brie[fly] boiling salted water (about 1 minute). Remove to a bowl wit[h] cold water to stop the cooking (keep the rest of the aspar[agus] stems for a stock or to be used in another dish).

■ Cook the pasta in a pot of boiling salted water until al d[ente] (about 8 minutes) and strain.

■ Heat the butter with the cream in a wide pot until melted. S[tir] the Parmesan cheese and garlic and mix until sauce thick[ens,] season with salt as needed. Add the pasta and asparagus tips [and] cook for 2 more minutes until pasta is well coated.

■ Apportion the pasta to serving plates, drizzle with the waln[ut oil] and sprinkle with the roasted walnuts and black pepper.

"MANY THINGS CAN STIMULATE THE PASSION
TO COOK: GOING TO THE MARKET, EATING
OUT OR A DESIRE TO USE A BEAUTIFUL
SERVING PLATE. BE INSPIRED."

VEGETARIAN

Serves 6

Heat the oil to 350 degrees F.

■ Cut the avocadoes in half, discard the pit and spoon the avocadoes to a cutting board. Dice avocadoes (small) and drizzle with the lime juice.

■ Mix in the chopped shallots, garlic and cumin and season well with salt and pepper. Check for flavor and correct seasoning if needed.

■ On a working surface, spread the egg roll skins working with one at a time to prevent them from drying, and spread 2-3 tablespoons of the avocado salad (allowing a half-inch space from the edge). Drain the sun-dried tomatoes and spread about 4-5 on the avocado.

■ Brush the edges of the egg roll skin with water and quickly fold about an inch from the side inwards, towards the filling. Use your thumbs to roll the side that is close to you toward the far end.

Roll gently to prevent stuffing from spilling out. Make sure the far end sticks to keep the rolls intact when frying.

■ Fry the rolls for about 2 minutes or until golden and crispy (if not completely fried after two minutes oil temperature was too low).

For the Dipping Sauce

■ Heat soy sauce, sugar and ginger in a saucepan until sugar dissolves. Add rice vinegar, Miso and scallions.

■ Cut the roll on the bias. Season the greens with a little olive oil and salt and pile a small amount in the middle of each serving plate. Lean the cut roll against the greens, pour dipping sauce into small ramekins and place on the plate. Serve immediately.

g roll skins
cadoes, ripe but not too soft
unce jar sun-dried tomatoes in oil (or sun-dried
toes, soaked in hot water for 3 minutes until soft)
lespoon lime juice
lic cloves, minced
llot, finely chopped
up chopped scallions
easpoon ground cumin
and pepper
r deep-frying (canola oil, peanut oil)
culin greens for garnish

the Dipping Sauce:
cup soy sauce
spoons sugar
lespoons rice vinegar
lespoons sliced scallions
lespoon Miso paste
lespoon minced ginger

EGGPLANT, PASTA & TAPANADE ROLL

Serves 6

2 medium eggplants
1 cup olive oil
3 cups back olives, pitted
4 anchovy fillets
2 garlic cloves
1 teaspoon cider vinegar
1 box lasagna sheets, cooked
1 avocado
Salt and pepper

Preheat oven to 375 degrees F.

Preparation – Eggplants:

■ Slice the eggplants about 1/8-inch thick, lengthwise.

■ Drizzle half cup of the oil on a baking sheet and place the eggplant on it. Drizzle the remaining oil on the eggplants and place in the oven for 20-25 minutes (rotate in the oven, if needed). Let cool before assembling.

Preparation – Tapanade:

■ Place the olives, anchovies and vinegar in a food processor. Puree for 1 minute and add the garlic; puree until the garlic is chopped, and season with salt. Puree again for 30 seconds.

■ Cut the avocado in half, remove the pit, spoon eac onto a cutting board and slice thickly.

■ Line the working surface with saran wrap. Mak rows of overlapping eggplant slices, 5 per row, overla 1/4 of an inch, one on top of the other. Place one lay the lasagna sheets on top and cover by spreading v nice even layer of the tapanade. Line with the avo slices.

■ Using both hands, roll the side close to you rotation, while disengaging from the saran wrap. Con to roll using the saran to help maintain the shape, b not roll saran wrap into a roulade. The final roulade v shaped into a log.

■ Refrigerate for 30 minutes. Before serving, slic edges one-inch thick and serve with a salad.

SAUTÉED GREEN AND YELLOW BEAN'
WITH SPICED ALMONDS AND
ROQUEFORT CHEESE
Serves 4-6

1 pound green beans, tips trimmed
1 pound wax (yellow) beans, tips trimmed
1 cup whole blanched almonds
1/2 teaspoon garlic powder
1/2 teaspoon onion powder
1/4 teaspoon cayenne pepper
1 tablespoon honey
2 shallots, chopped
2 garlic cloves, chopped
Salt and pepper
1/2 pound Roquefort cheese (if strong flavor is not
desired substitute with a mild goat cheese)
2 tablespoons sherry wine vinegar
3 tablespoons extra virgin olive oil

at the oven to 350 degrees F.

ing a big pot with water to a boil and salt the water
ously. Cook the green beans for about 3-4 minutes
emove to a bowl with ice water. Cook the yellow beans
minutes and remove to a bowl with ice water.

I a small baking dish. Mix the almonds with the honey
eason with salt, cayenne, onion and garlic powder.

Transfer the almonds to the baking dish and bake for 15
minutes until golden. Let cool.

■ Heat the oil in a wide sauté pan and sauté the onion
and garlic for 1 minute. Add the yellow and green beans
and sauté over a high flame for 3-4 minutes. Season with
salt and pepper and transfer to a big bowl. While hot, toss
with the almonds, vinegar and Roquefort cheese. Serve
warm.

MUSHROOM & PARMESAN RISOTTO CAKES
Serves 4-6

Preparation - Mushrooms:

■ Remove the stem of the mushrooms and slice them. Heat the olive oil in a wide sauté pan and sauté the shallots for two minutes; add the mushrooms and cook for 5-7 minutes over a high flame.

■ Add Vermouth, thyme and cook until almost evaporated, about 3 minutes, season with salt and pepper. Remove from the pan to a strainer to get rid of excess liquids.

■ Heat the stock in a large saucepan over medium heat until it comes to a boil. Reduce to a low heat, keeping the stock at a steady simmer.

■ Heat the oil in heavy-bottomed saucepan over medium heat. Add the shallots, and cook until translucent, about 4 minutes. Add the rice, and cook, stirring with a wooden spoon, until the rice is coated in the oil and the kernels are translucent, about 3 minutes.

■ Add the wine to the rice, and cook, stirring, until the wine is absorbed. Ladle 3/4 cup of the hot stock in the rice, stirring constantly until most of the liquid h been absorbed, and the mixture is just thick enough leave a clear wake when a line is drawn through about 3 minutes. Continue adding stock in this mann (about 3/4 cup at a time), stirring constantly, until all th stock evaporates and the rice is fully cooked an suspended in a liquid that resembles heavy crea about 20 minutes.

■ Remove risotto from heat, add cheese, mushroom and parsley, stirring until melted and combined, about minute. Season with salt, pepper and truffle oil. Let co

■ Heat the oil to 350 degrees F and line a plate wi paper towels.

■ When cooled, form small balls with wet hands prevent the risotto from sticking. Roll the balls breadcrumbs and fry for 2 minutes until light gold and crisp. Remove from the oil to the lined plate. Ser with green salad or roasted vegetables.

8-10 cups vegetable stock
3 tablespoons extra virgin olive oil
2 large shallots, finely chopped
1 1/2 cups Arborio rice
1/2 cup dry white wine
1 cup freshly grated Parmigiano cheese
1/4 cup chopped fresh flat-leaf parsley
2 large shallots, finely minced
1 1/4 pounds (20 ounces) mixed mushrooms (cremini, button, portobello and/or shiitake)
3 tablespoons olive oil
2 tablespoons dry Vermouth
1 tablespoon fresh thyme leaves
Coarse salt and freshly ground black pepper
1 teaspoon truffle oil (optional)
Breadcrumbs
Oil for deep-frying

"FOOD IS MUCH MORE THAN NECESSITY. IT HAS A SOCIAL ROLE TO BRING FAMILIES AND PEOPLE TOGETHER."

FISH

GRILLED HALIBUT WITH BRAISED ENDIVE AND BUTTERNUT SQUASH SAUCE OVER POTATO ROSTI

Serves 4

Preparation - Sauce:

■ Warm the olive oil and sweat the onions and garlic in a big pot until the onions are translucent. Add the diced butternut squash and sauté for 3-4 minutes.

■ Season with salt and pepper and add the vegetable stock. The liquids should just cover the butternut squash. Bring to a boil and reduce to medium-low heat. Let simmer covered for 35-40 minutes until the butternut squash is very tender.

■ With an emulsifier blender (or in a food processor) puree the sauce to an even, smooth texture. Add the heavy cream and bring to a boil over low heat.

Remove from the heat and taste for seasoning. Thinly basil leaves and mix in.

■ Cut the fish into 8-ounce portions and refrigerated until needed.

Preparation - Braised Endives:

■ Slice the endives 1/4-inch thick, lengthwise, kee the shape of the endive. Pour 3 tablespoons water in inch sauté pan; arrange the endive slices (do not c the pan) and sprinkle with 3 tablespoons brown s Bring to a quick boil then reduce to a very low heat cover. Let cook for about 10 minutes until the "hea the endive slices are soft and the color is light br

2 pounds halibut fillet
4 endives
3 tablespoons dark brown sugar
3 tablespoons water
1 small butternut squash, peeled, seeded and diced 1/2 inch thick
1 medium onion, diced
4 garlic cloves, chopped
1 cup heavy cream
2 tablespoons olive oil
3-4 cups vegetable stock or water
10 basil leaves, washed and dried
7 Idaho potatoes
1/2 cup vegetable oil
Salt and pepper

...ove from the pan and cook another batch if needed. ...o warm.

...paration - Rosti:

...eel and grate the potatoes (can be done in a food ...essor). Place 3 handfuls in a towel and squeeze to ...ove excess liquids; place in a new mixing bowl and ...at with the remaining potatoes. Season the potatoes ...with salt and pepper.

...eat the oil in two nonstick pans until hot, but not ...king. Layer the potatoes evenly in the pans (not thicker ...1/2 inch) and cook over medium heat for 5-7 minutes ...the rosti is fully cooked. With the help of a plate or a

flat tray flip the rosti to the other side (add a little more oil if needed) and cook for an additional 7 minutes. Remove from the heat and keep warm.

■ Heat a grilling pan, or griddle. Brush the fish lightly with olive oil and season with salt and pepper. Grill skin side up for 3-4 minutes then flip sides and grill for 4-5 additional minutes. Cooking can be finished in a preheated oven (375 degrees F).

■ Slice the rosti into thin triangles with a knife or pizza wheel to create 2 per servings. Place the triangles in a serving plate, overlap 4 slices of the endive on the plate and top with the fish. Ladle the sauce around and serve.

GRILLED SEA BASS OVER BAKED SWEET POTATOES AND SAUTÉED SPINACH IN RED WINE SAUCE

Serves 4

1 bottle red wine (Merlot or Cabernet)	2 pounds sea bass
1 medium onion	3 tablespoons olive oil
2 carrots	3 medium sweet potatoes
1 celery stalk	1/3 cup olive oil
5 garlic cloves, crushed	Fresh rosemary
Fresh parsley	Salt and pepper
Fresh thyme	2 bunches spinach leaves washed and dried
Salt and pepper	3 garlic cloves, sliced
2 ounces butter to finish the sauce	4 ounces butter

Preheat oven to 375 degrees F.

Preparation - Sauce:

■ Slice the onion, carrots and celery. Heat 2 tablespoons of olive oil in a saucepot and sauté the vegetables for 2 minutes. Add the wine and herbs and bring to a boil. Reduce to a low heat and let reduce by three quarters. Strain and set aside for use later.

■ Slice the sweet potatoes, thinly. Overlap them baking pan, drizzle with olive oil, season with salt pepper, and sprinkle with fresh rosemary. Cover with foil and place in the oven. Bake for 30 minutes then rem foil and bake for an additional 15-20 minutes.

■ Score the skin side of the fish lightly.

ush the fish fillets with olive oil and season with salt
epper. Heat a grilling pan or a griddle until very hot
lace the fish flesh side down on the pan. Grill for 1
e and turn 90 degrees to create a crisscross mark.
nother minute and flip to the skin side for 2 minutes.
ng can be finished in a preheated oven.

elt the butter in a sauté pan, sauté the garlic for 30
ds, and add the spinach. Season with salt and pepper
ook for 1 minute. Remove from the heat.

■ To finish the sauce, heat a sauté pan and pour in the
reduced wine allowing to boil for 20 seconds. Add 2
ounces of butter, mixing constantly, until the sauce
thickens and has a rich texture.

■ Arrange 6 slices of the sweet potatoes; place the fish
on top, followed by the spinach, and drizzle around with
sauce.

PAN-SEARED TILAPIA OVER PEAR AND MINT RISOTTO IN BALSAMIC REDUCTION SAUCE AND GRILLED SCALLIONS

Serves 4

4 6-8 ounce tilapia fillets
2 ounces butter or olive oil
1 small onion, diced
2 garlic cloves, minced
2 ounces butter
2 cups Arborio rice
1/2 cup dry white wine
1 1/2 quarts vegetable stock
1/2 cup pear nectar

3 pears peeled and diced
1/2 cup chopped mint leaves
Salt and pepper
1 bottle good balsamic vinegar
2 shallots, chopped
8 scallions
1 tablespoon olive oil
Salt and pepper

Heat the oil in a high saucepan and sauté the chopped shallots for 2 minutes. Add the balsamic vinegar, bring to a boil and reduce to a simmer. Let cook until the balsamic is thick enough to coat the back of a spoon (about 25 minutes) and reduced by two thirds. Keep warm.

In a big wide pot, melt the butter and sauté the onions and garlic for 2 minutes. Add the rice and the white wine mixing constantly. When liquids are gone add 1 cup of the vegetable stock at a time, mixing until liquids are reduced. Continue until rice is fully cooked about 20-25 minutes. Add the pears and the mint, followed by the pear nectar. Season well with salt and pepper and cook for 5 additional minutes.

Remove from the heat and keep warm.

Brush the scallions with the olive oil and season well with salt and pepper. Grill in a grill pan or over a griddle for 2-3 minutes on each side. Keep in a warm place to continue cooking (can be done in a 350 degrees F preheated oven).

Season the fish well and sauté in the butter, in a preheated sauté pan, 3 minutes on each side. Place 3-4 tablespoons of the risotto in the middle of a serving plate and top with the fish. Drizzle around with balsamic reduction sauce and place 2 scallions in an X over the fish.

FILLET OF SOLE IN BROWN SAGE AND CAPERS BUTTER OVER WHITE BEAN PUREE AND SAUTÉED ARUGULA

Serves 4

Place the lemon zest in a small baking sheet or pan in a hot place (on top of the stove) or in a 120 degree F preheated oven for about 1-2 hours until dry.

Preparation – White Bean Puree

■ Place the beans, water, garlic and onion in a pot. Bring to a boil and discard the white foam. Lower to medium/low heat, add the herbs and season well with salt and pepper. Cook covered until beans are very soft (about 45-60 minutes). Remove the herbs and drain, letting the beans sit in the colander for 5 minutes. Puree, using a food mill or a food processor. If using a food processor puree for a short time to avoid sticky texture. Check for seasoning.

■ In a heated, nonstick pan, add 1 ounce of butter. Season the fish with salt and pepper and cook for 1-2 minutes on each side. Remove the fish from the pan and add the rest of the butter. When fully melted, add the sage and capers (be careful, wet capers will cause butter to splatter). Cook until butter turns brown.

■ Place 3 tablespoons of the white bean puree on the side of a serving plate, lean fillet of sole against it and drizzle with the butter sauce. Cook the chopped garlic in a buttered pan for 30 seconds, add the arugula and season with salt. Cook for 1 minute until arugula is cooked (this can be done in advance and arugula can be quickly reheated). Place on top of the fish and serve.

4 fillets of sole
6 ounces butter
4-5 fresh sage leaves
Zest from 2 lemons
(optional)
1/2 cup capers, drained
2 cups of white navy beans,
soaked in water overnight
and washed (or two cans of
navy beans and 8 cloves of
roasted garlic)
8 garlic cloves (not if using
the roasted ones with the
canned beans)
1 small onion, diced
2 strings fresh thyme
1 bay leaf
6 cups water
Salt and pepper
2 bunches arugula, washed
and dried
1 garlic clove, minced

GROUPER FILLETS OVER EGGPLANT CAVIAR, WARM BALSAMIC VINAIGRETTE AND POTATO SHOE STRINGS

Serves 4

Preparation - Caviar:

■ Poke the eggplants with a fork. Roast the eggplants over the stove or a grill, turning them every few minutes, until the skin is lightly burnt and the eggplants are very soft (about 15 minutes each). Remove from the heat and place in a colander in the sink to get rid of excess liquids and cool.

■ When cooled, but still warm, peel the skin off using your hands or a small knife. Save a small piece of the burnt skin. Puree 2/3 of the eggplant, garlic, oil and

lemon juice in a blender and season well with sa pepper. Correct seasoning as needed. Add the p the remaining eggplant, the saved burnt eggplar and the Tabasco and puree for a short time so th texture will be a little chunky. Keep warm.

Preparation - Vinaigrette:

■ Sauté the shallot in 1 tablespoon of the olive 1 minute, until translucent. Add the balsamic vineg

4 8-ounce grouper fillets
2 tablespoons olive oil
2 medium firm eggplants
1/4 cup extra virgin olive oil
2 garlic cloves
Juice of 1 lemon
1/2 cup parsley leaves, washed and dried
1/2 teaspoon Tabasco sauce (optional)

1/3 cup high quality balsamic vinegar
1 cup extra virgin olive oil
1 shallot, chopped
1 teaspoon honey
Salt and Pepper
2 Idaho potatoes
Canola oil, enough for deep-frying

; lower the
and mix well until the
fully dissolves. Transfer to a mixing bowl
hile whisking add the olive oil very slowly for a
exture. Season with salt and pepper and check for
If too bland add a little more balsamic. Keep in a
warm water.

el the potatoes and slice thinly, lengthwise. Cut
like strings (use a mandolin if you have one). Heat
to 350 degrees F. Deep-fry the potato strings
golden and crisp. Do not overcrowd the

frying pot; fry in two
batches, if needed. Transfer
potatoes to plate lined with paper towels using a
slotted spoon. Sprinkle with salt.

■ Season the fish with salt and pepper. Heat the
oil in a sauté pan and cook the fish for about 3-4
minutes on each side. Place 3 tablespoons of the
eggplant caviar in the middle of a serving plate
and arrange the fish on top. Top with the fried potato
strings and drizzle around with the warm vinaigrette.
Serve immediately.

Serves 4

4 Tilapia fillets
1 package cornmeal
2 eggs
Flour
1/3 cup oil
2 leeks
3 red peppers
4 medium Yukon gold potatoes or Idaho potatoes
6-8 cups vegetable stock
Salt and pepper
Fresh thyme

Preparation - Fillets:

■ Place the flour, eggs and cornmeal in 3 different plates. Season the cornmeal with salt and pepper. Beat the eggs.

■ Dredge the tilapia fillets in the flour, shake, dredge in the beaten eggs and transfer to the cornmeal plate. The fish should be thoroughly coated.

■ Pour oil in a sauté pan (oil should be very hot but not smoky). Place the fish in the pan and sauté each side for 2 minutes. Remove from the pan. Place some of the ragout on a serving plate with the tilapia on top and garnish with young leaves salad or chopped scallions.

Preparation - Ragout:

■ Place the oil in a pot and heat up. Put the red in the pot and sauté for 2-3 minutes until slightly brown.

■ Add the leeks and stir together.

■ Place the potatoes inside the pot, and stir togeth  cook for 2-3 minutes.

■ Add vegetable stock and the thyme and cook c heat until potatoes are soft, but not falling apart.

■ Season with salt and pepper and keep it in a w place until served.

CRISPY BLACK BASS WITH FENNEL JAM AND SAFFRON VINAIGRETTE

Serves 4

SEE

■ Combine the fennel, orange juice (minus the pulp), honey, and currants in a shallow, heavy-bottomed pan and simmer over low heat until the liquid is reduced by half and the fennel is very tender, about 30 minutes. Drain the fennel, season with salt and pepper and set aside to cool.

■ Place the 1/2 cup orange juice in a small, sta still saucepan and warm over medium heat ur juices are released, adding water, if necessa prevent scorching. Add the saffron, cover and tu the heat. Combine the saffron and orange mixture with 4 tablespoons of the olive oi champagne vinegar, salt and pepper and whis for a thick texture. Set aside.

ounce fillets of black bass 2
s of fennel, sliced 1/4-inch thick
s fresh orange juice + additional 1/2 cup
cup honey
cup currants
er salt and freshly ground black
er
easpoon saffron threads
lespoons extra virgin olive oil
tablespoons champagne
gar
up finely chopped flat-leaf
ey
virgin olive oil, for drizzling

eat the remaining 2 tablespoons of olive oil in a
uté pan over high heat until smoking. Score the
f each fish fillet twice and season well with salt
epper. Place in a pan, skin side down and cook
crispy on the skin side, about 3 minutes. Turn
nish cooking on the flesh side, about 2 more
es.

■ Meanwhile, in a sauté pan, heat the fennel jam
over high heat until warmed through. Stir in the
parsley. Place one portion of the jam on each of four
dinner plates. Place a fillet on top, spoon vinaigrette
around, and drizzle with the oil. Serve immediately.

BAKED CODSTEAKS OVER CHICKPEA PANCAKES IN ROASTED GARLIC AND GRILLED TOMATO SAUCE

Serves 4

4 seven-ounce cod steaks
2 garlic heads
8 ripe tomatoes
1 small onion
2 stems fresh thyme
1 stem fresh rosemary

1/2 cup chopped fresh parsley leaves
2 bay leaves
2+2 tablespoons olive oil
2 cups chickpea flour
1 teaspoon salt

1/2 teaspoon ground cu
1/4 teaspoon cayenne p
1/2 teaspoon turmeric p
1 1/2 cups water
Vegetable oil to coat fry

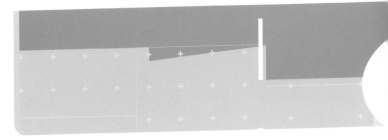

eat oven to 375 degrees F.

eel the garlic, place in aluminum foil, drizzle with
oil and bake for 30 minutes until the cloves are very
er. Grill 6 tomatoes on a hot grilling pan on all sides,
t 5 minutes.

eel and dice the onion. Heat 2 tablespoons olive oil
saucepan, add the onion and sauté for 2 minutes.
the tomatoes, bay leaves and 1 thyme stem and
for 10 minutes over medium heat. Season with salt
epper. Discard the bay leaves and thyme stem and
e the sauce in a food processor. Add the garlic and
ess for 2 minutes; strain the sauce.

hile the sauce is cooking season the fish steaks
salt and pepper. Slice the remaining 2 tomatoes and

line a baking sheet with the slices. Place fish on top of
the tomatoes and sprinkle with fresh thyme and
rosemary leaves. Cover with aluminum foil and bake for
15-20 minutes.

Preparation - Chickpea Pancakes:

■ Mix all dry ingredients together in a food processor
or bowl. Add 1 1/2 cups water and blend well. Use a
large serving spoon to drop mixture into oiled frying pan.
Fry on both sides over a medium flame about 1 to 2
minutes, or until golden brown. Keep warm.

■ Place pancakes on a serving plate with the fish next
to the pancake and top with the sauce. Garnish with the
chopped parsley leaves.

TUNA BURGERS WITH ONION RINGS

Serves 4

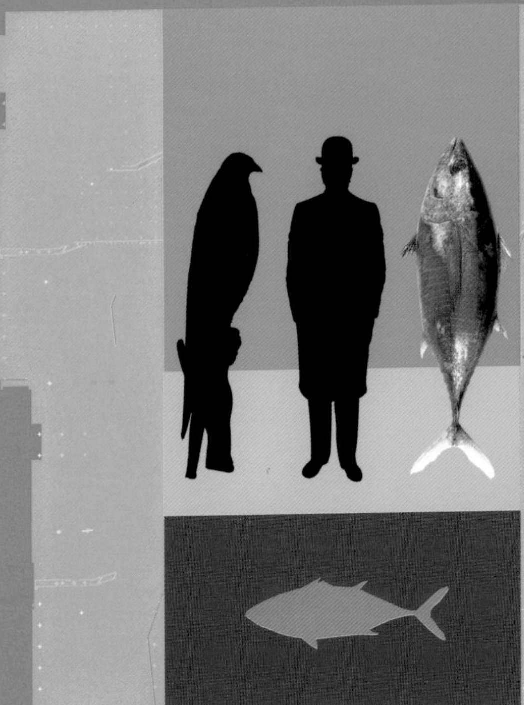

2 pounds tuna
1 small onion, choppe
2 garlic cloves, mince
3 tablespoons olive oi
1 tablespoon soy sauc
1 teaspoon sesame oi
(optional)
1/2 cup chopped pars
Salt and pepper
Burger buns
Mayonnaise
Tomato, sliced
Iceberg lettuce
2 medium onions
Wondra flour
Oil for deep-frying

■ Cut the tuna into small dices and mix with the rest of the ingredients. Season with salt and pepper.

■ Heat 1/4 cup of oil in a big sauté pan. Form 4 burgers from the seasoned tuna "throwing" them from one hand to the other to "punch" the air out. Place them in the pan and sauté 3 minutes on each side. For well-done burgers, finish the cooking in a preheated oven.

■ Heat the frying oil to 350 degrees F.

■ Slice the onions thinly on a mandolin or with a sharp knife. In a mixing bowl, toss them with the Wondra flour then get rid of excess flour. Place the onion slices in the oil and fry them for 1 minute until lightly golden. Transfer to a plate lined with paper towel and sprinkle them with salt.

■ Serve on a burger bun with mayo, tomato and lettuce while hot, with onion rings on the side, or placed on top.

"LEARN TO LOVE FOOD BY TRYING NEW
THINGS. BE CURIOUS."

POULTRY

MAPLE AND GARLIC ROASTED CHICKE
OVER HERBED PANCAKE AND SAUTÉ
BROCCOLI RABE
Serves 4

3 pounds chicken, quartered
Salt and pepper
1/2 cup Hoi Sin sauce
1/3 cup Canola oil
2/3 cup maple syrup
12 garlic cloves, peeled
1/2 cup white wine or chicken stock
2 tablespoons Miso paste

For the pancake:
8 ounces cake flour
1 teaspoon salt
1 tablespoon baking powder

2 large eggs
2 cups soy milk
2 tablespoons chopped parsley
2 tablespoons chopped mint
1 tablespoon chopped sage
2 ounces margarine, melted
1/2 cup olive oil

1 large bunch broccoli rabe
2 tablespoons extra virgin olive oil
2 large garlic cloves, smashed and cut into
slices
Coarse salt and freshly ground black pepper

heat oven to 375 degrees F.

Using your hands, rub the Hoi Sin sauce under skin of the chicken, gently, to avoid tearing. ason the chicken parts with salt and pepper.

Heat the oil in a wide sauté pan and sear the cken for 3-4 minutes on each side, until golden d crisp. Remove to a baking dish.

Add the wine to the pan and scorch the bottom h a wooden spoon. Add the maple, Miso and lic cloves. Taste for flavor. If too sweet, add a little re wine and Miso; if too salty, add a little more ple syrup. Season with salt and pepper.

Pour the sauce over the chicken parts and cover h aluminum foil. Bake in oven for 45 minutes; nove the foil and bake 15-20 additional minutes.

eparation – Pancake:

In a mixing bowl combine flour, salt and baking wder. Mix well.

■ In a second bowl combine milk, eggs and margarine. Mix well. Add the liquid ingredients to the dry ingredients and mix until combined. Add the herbs, DON'T OVERMIX.

■ Heat a non-stick pan and grease it lightly with olive oil. With a two-ounce ladle, measure portions of the pancake batter onto the pan. Fry the pancakes until the tops are full of bubbles and begin to look dry. Turn and brown the other side.

■ Trim 2 inches off the bottom of the broccoli rabe stalks, and discard. In a large skillet, heat the olive oil over medium heat. Add the garlic slices and cook until fragrant and lightly golden, about 20 seconds. Add the broccoli rabe and sauté until it is coated in the garlic oil, about 2 minutes. Season with salt.

■ Place 2 pancakes on each serving plate, place one of the chicken parts on top and drizzle with sauce. Top with the broccoli rabe and serve.

CRISPY DUCK BREAST WITH MANGO RELISH AND YUCCA FRIES

Serves 4

■ Peel the mangoes, cut the fruit around the pit and dice to one-eighth of an inch. Place in a big mixing bowl and mix with the rest of the ingredients. Check for flavor. If too spicy add more sugar.

Heat the frying oil to 350 degrees F.

■ Peel the yucca and slice, paper thin, on a mandolin or with a very sharp knife. Fry in batches until

golden and crisp. Transfer to a plate lined
paper towel and season with salt while hot.

■ Score the duck fat (skin) with a sharp
Heat a heavy pan and place the duck, skin
down to melt the fat, about 10 minutes
medium heat. Remove the breasts, season wit
and pepper and get rid of the excess fat (ca

duck breasts with skin, about 8
nces each
mangoes, ripe but not too soft
small red onion, diced small
garlic clove, minced
teaspoon chopped fresh ginger
tablespoons light brown sugar
2 teaspoon curry powder
2 teaspoon cayenne pepper
tablespoons lime juice
2 tablespoons extra virgin olive oil
1/2 cup chopped mint leaves
11/2 pounds yucca
Vegetable oil for deep-frying
Salt and pepper

n the refrigerator after cooling). Return
easts to the pan, skin side up, and cook
4 minutes to a medium-rare temperature.

ce the duck breast on a serving plate,
3-4 tablespoons of the relish next to it
p with the fries.

CORNMEAL CRUSTED CHICKEN SCALLOPINI OVER LEGUME HASH IN ROASTED RED PEPPER SAUCE

Serves 4

8 chicken cutlets (4ounces each),
pounded thin
2 eggs, beaten
1 cup yellow cornmeal
Salt and pepper
1/3 cup olive oil
1 red onion, diced small
2 cups fresh corn kernels (or frozen and
thawed)
2 cups kidney beans, washed and
drained
1 cup lima beans (if frozen,
thaw before using)
4 garlic cloves, sliced
3 tablespoons Canola oil
1/3 cup chopped fresh mint
leaves
Salt
1/2 teaspoon ground coriander
1/4 teaspoon cayenne pepper
1 tablespoon green tabasco sauce

For the Sauce:

2 shallots, chopped
2 garlic cloves, minced
1/4 cup olive oil
4 roasted red peppers, peeled and sliced
1 cup chicken stock
Salt and pepper
1/2 teaspoon sweet paprika
1/2 teaspoon fresh thyme leaves
1/2 cup chopped scallions (green part
only) for garnish

Preparation - Sauce:

■ Heat the olive oil in a saucepan and add the shallots
and garlic. Add the thyme and paprika, sauté for 1 minute,
then toss in the roasted peppers. Cook for 2-3 minutes
and add the vegetable stock. Cook over high heat for 5
minutes and remove from the heat.

■ Season well with salt and pepper and chec[k]
flavors. If needed, add more paprika or garlic. Pure[e]
sauce and strain it for a smooth shiny texture. Keep [warm]

■ In a wide sauté pan heat the oil for the legume [hash]
Sauté the onion and garlic for 1 minute, followed b[y]
fresh corn kernels and the lima beans. Sauté for 2 m[inutes]
and add the kidney beans.

...ason with the cayenne, coriander and salt. Check ...or. Remove from heat and mix in the mint leaves ...reen tabasco (only if you serve immediately, ...ise keep the hash until serving, heat again and ...eason).

... the salt and black pepper with the cornmeal. ... the chicken scallopini in the beaten egg and then in the cornmeal mixture. Heat the oil in a large sauté pan and fry for 2 minutes on each side until lightly golden and crisp.

■ Place 4 tablespoons of the legume hash in the middle of a serving plate, lean 2 scallopini against it and drizzle around with sauce. Sprinkle with chopped chives.

ROASTED GARLIC STUFFED CHICKEN BREAST OVER FENNEL CONFIT IN SAFFRON COCONUT MILK SAUCE AND BABY LEAF SALAD

Serves 4

4 chicken breasts
12 garlic cloves
Extra virgin olive oil
2 fennel bulbs (leaves & stalks discarded)
Salt and black pepper
1 tablespoon fresh thyme leaves
2 shallots, chopped
2/3 cup dry white wine
1 can coconut milk
A pinch of saffron

For the Baby Leaf Salad:
1 cup baby spinach
1/2 cup baby arugula
1/2 cup mash
1/2 cup red alfalfa sprouts
1/4 cup tarragon leaves
1 teaspoon lemon juice
Extra virgin olive oil

...eat oven to 275 degrees F.

...With a Japanese mandolin (or a very sharp knife)
...e the fennel into thin, even slices. Arrange
...el slices on a baking sheet, drizzle with oil and
...on with salt and pepper. Sprinkle the thyme
...es and cover with aluminum foil. Bake in the
...n for 45 minutes or until the fennel is very tender
...not falling apart.

■ While the fennel is baking, peel the garlic cloves,
drizzle with oil and wrap in foil. Place in the oven for
30 minutes or until the garlic is tender. Remove
from the oven.

■ Clean the chicken breast and cut it in half. With
a sharp paring knife create a pocket in each one of
them. Stuff them with the roasted garlic cloves (6
each) and seal with a toothpick.

...eat 2 tablespoons of olive oil in a sauté pan.
...hot (but not smoky) place chicken breast in
...an. Sear each side for 2 minutes to a golden
...Remove from the pan and place in the oven
...minutes.

...d 2 more tablespoons of oil and sauté the
...ts for 1 minute. Add the white wine and let
...er for 5 seconds while scrubbing the pan. Add
...oconut milk and reduce to medium heat. Add
...affron and season with salt and pepper.

■ Mix the greens in a small mixing bowl, season
with the lemon juice, olive oil, salt and pepper.

■ Arrange the fennel confit in the middle of the
plate. On a cutting board, cut the chicken breast on
a bias and fan over the fennel. Circle with the sauce
and top with the baby leaf salad.

GRILLED DUCK BREAST OVER CRISPY DICED POTATOES WITH MUSHROOM STEW

Serves 4

For the sauce:

For the stew...

4 duck breasts, 7 ounces each, skin removed and sliced1/8-inch thick, on the bias
Salt and pepper
1 tablespoon olive oil
1 Vidalia onion (or other sweet onion), halved and thinly sliced
4-5 Yukon gold potatoes, peeled and diced (1/4 inch)
1/4 cup olive oil
Salt and pepper
5 ounces Button mushrooms, sliced
5 ounces Shiitake mushrooms, stem removed, sliced
5 ounces Cremini mushrooms, sliced
3 ounces Black Trumpet mushrooms (if sandy, wash gently)
3 ounce dried Porcini mushrooms or 5 ounces fresh ones
4 ounce Chanterelle mushrooms
4 garlic cloves, lightly crushed
2 shallots, thinly sliced
1 1/2 cups dark beef stock or chicken stock
3 tablespoons olive oil
2 tablespoons good brand cognac
1 sprig thyme
2 sprigs tarragon
2 sprigs parsley
1/2 teaspoon fennel seed
2 bay leaves
Cheesecloth
Twine
Sea salt and pepper
1/3 cup chopped fresh ba leaves
Truffle oil

ace the potato dices in a pot and cover with cold
Add salt. Bring the water to a boil. Drain and
er the potatoes into a bowl with ice water to stop the
ng. Drain again and let sit for 5 minutes to get rid of
s water.

using dried mushrooms, soak them in hot water
should cover the mushrooms) for 7 minutes. Drain
ep the water aside.

aration - Stew:

th a short, sharp knife, cut the tip of the stem of the
erelle mushrooms and gently peel the outside layer
stems. If large, cut them into quarters. Place all
and seasonings in the cheesecloth and tie with a
Heat the olive oil in a wide saucepot and sauté the
slices and garlic for 1 minute. Add the brandy,
the pan away from you to avoid a flame if flambé.
ne Shiitake, Cremini and Button mushrooms and
while stirring for 1 minute. Add the dried Porcini and
anterelle and season well with salt and pepper. Add

the stock, 1/2 cup from the dried mushroom liquids and
the herbs and cook, uncovered, over a low-medium flame,
for 30 minutes. Immediately before serving mix in the basil
leaves.

Preparation - Potatoes:

■ Heat 1 tablespoon of the oil in a wide sauté pan
(preferably a non-stick one) and sauté the onions until
golden brown, about 5-7 minutes. Remove from the pan
and set aside. Heat the rest of the oil until very hot and
add the potatoes. Sauté them, mixing occasionally, until
golden and crisp. Add the onions to the potatoes and
sauté for 1 minute. Season well with salt and pepper and
place in the middle of a serving plate.

■ Brush the duck slices with the oil and season with salt
and pepper. Heat a grill pan or a griddle and when very
hot grill the duck slices 30 seconds on each side. Fan the
slices against the potatoes and spoon the mushroom stew
around. Drizzle a few drops of the truffle oil on top of the
duck (it is very strong in flavor) and serve.

BUTTERNUT SQUASH BOATS WITH TURKEY STUFFING, SAUTÉED SWISS CHARD "LASAGNA" IN CHICKEN REDUCTION SAUCE

Serves 4

Preheat oven to 350 degrees F.

- Cut the squash in half, lengthwise, and use a spoon to discard the seeds.

- In a sauté pan, heat the chicken fat until clear and sauté the garlic and onion for 1

minute
until onion is
translucent. Keep the pan aside to cool.

- Mix the turkey meat with the seasoning in a mixing bowl. In a separate bowl, mix the cream with the eggs. Add the onion, garlic and fat to the meat. Combine well and add the egg mixture. Stir just until combined. To taste for flavor, cook a small portion of the meat and season accordingly.

- Stuff the middle of the halved squash (where the seeds were) with the stuffing and place in a deep baking dish. Sprinkle with salt and pepper and pour 2 cups of the chicken stock into the pan. Add the sage and cover with foil. Bake for 45 minutes then remove foil and bake for 15-20 additional minutes. Remove

from the oven. Add the liquids from the pan reduction sauce.

Preparation - Sauce:

Heat the oil in a saucepot and sauté the vege for 3-4 minutes. Add the stock and scor bottom of the pot. Bring to a bo reduce to a simmer. Place aromatics in the chee and tie well. Pla cloth in the p simmer and by 2/3 un sauce is brown (abo minutes).

- Meanw bring a pot wit to a boil. Salt the and cook the l leaves al dente (fresh about 2-3 minutes; dry pasta ab 10). Drain and toss with a little olive oil t sticking. Spread on a tray.

- In a wide sauté pan, heat the 1/2 of the oil Swiss chard. Add 1/2 of the garlic and sau green Swiss chard for 1 minute. Season with s pepper and remove from the pan to a straine rid of excess liquids. Repeat with the red Swiss

- On a serving plate, alternate the lasagna with the red and green chard to create "fre lasagna." Cut each boat in half, lengthwise (op careful not to take the stuffing out, and lean the lasagna. Spoon the sauce around and s with tarragon leaves.

dium butternut squash
pounds ground turkey

lespoons chicken or
 fat
dium onion, diced small
lic cloves, minced
gs + 1 yolk
cup non-dairy heavy
m
easpoon ground
ard seeds
 of nutmeg
 chili pepper
ig sage
nch green chard, washed,
e part removed
nch red Swiss chard,
ed, white part removed
und fresh lasagna leaves
ackage lasagna leaves
lespoons olive oil
lic cloves, chopped
 and pepper
 quarts chicken stock at
 temperature
cup diced onion
cup peeled and diced
t
cup diced celery
secloth
igs thyme
igs tarragon
igs parsley
 leaf
lespoons Canola oil
cup fresh tarragon leaves

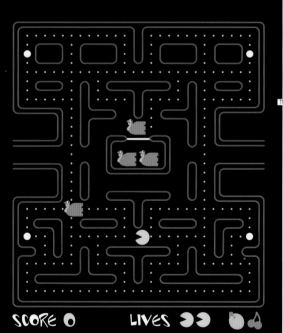

SCORE 0   LIVES

GRILLED QUAIL WITH BALSAMIC AN
HONEY OVER SPINACH RISOTTO AN
BRAISED LEEKS
Serves 4

Preheat oven to 375 degrees F.

■ Mix the balsamic vinegar with the honey and thyme sprigs. Rub the quails well with salt and pepper and place them in the marinade. Transfer to a dish that will fit all and let marinate in the refrigerator for at least 2 hours (up to 12 hours).

■ Place the leeks in a baking pan. Mix the wine and stock in a small bowl and pour over the leeks. Season with salt and pepper and cover with aluminum foil. Braise in the oven for 30 minutes. Remove foil and braise for 15-20 additional minutes until leeks are very soft and golden. Keep the liquids.

Preparation – Risotto:

■ Heat the margarine in a wide sauté pan until melted. Add the spinach leaves and season with salt and pepper. Cook over medium high flame until spinach is soft and dark green.

■ Remove from the pan and spread on a baking sheet for faster cooling. When cool, ground the spinach to a dark green, smooth texture in a blender or a food processor.

■ In a big wide pot, heat the oil and sauté the onions and garlic for 2 minutes. Add the rice and the white wine, mixing constantly. When liquids evaporate, add one cup of the chicken stock at a time. Continue

mixing until liquids evap
Continue until rice is fully c
about 18-20 minutes. Add
spinach puree and cream. S
well with salt and pepper and
for 5 additional minutes. Re
from the heat but keep warm.

■ Heat a griddle or a wide gri
Remove the quails from
marinade and pat dry. Brush
with olive oil and grill, skir
down, for 5 minutes. Turn ove
grill for 3 additional minutes.
half.

■ Put 5 tablespoons of the ris
a middle of a serving plate, cro
two halves against the risotte
top with two leeks. Drizzle a
with some of the leek braising
and serve.

■ 4 quails or squabs, about 1 pound each, backbone and breastbone removed ■ 1 bottle good bals
■ 8 leeks, white part only, well washed ■ 1/2 cup chicken stock ■ 2/3 cups semi sweet white wine
rice ■ 1/2 cup dry white wine ■ 1 1/2 quarts chicken stock ■ 1/3 cup non-dairy cream ■ 3

119

egar ■ 2/3 cup lavender honey ■ 4 sprigs thyme ■ Salt and pepper
mall onion, diced ■ 2 garlic cloves, minced ■ 1/4 cup olive oil ■ 2 cups Arborio
ach leaves, washed and dried ■ 1 tablespoon margarine ■ Salt and pepper

"FOOD EMBRACES ELEMENTS FROM OUR PAST. IT IS A PART OF OUR HISTORY AS A BEING, A FAMILY OR A NATION. IT IS FUNDAMENTAL IN CREATING CHERISHED MEMORIES."

MEAT

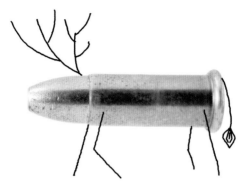

ORANGE AND COGNAC BEEF STEW OVER EGG NOODLES

Serves 4

3 pounds hanger steak, trimmed and cut into
1-inch cubes
1/2 cup flour
4 tablespoons Canola oil
2 onions, thinly sliced
2 cloves garlic, smashed and minced
1 pound Cremini mushrooms, quartered
1 cup red wine (Merlot or Cabernet)
4 tablespoons tomato paste
4 carrots, peeled and sliced into 1/4-inch
rounds
1 sprig fresh rosemary
1 sprig fresh sage
2 sprigs fresh thyme
1/4 cup good quality cognac or brandy
Juice of 1 orange, plus 2 strips of zest
Olive oil
Salt and pepper
1 pound flat egg noodles
3 tablespoons extra virgin olive oil
1/2 cup chopped chives
16 orange fillets for garnish (unsweetened
mandarin oranges or fresh)

■ Season steak with salt and pepper and toss with the flour. Get rid of the excess flour. In a large, deep, heavy pot, heat Canola oil. Add meat to the pot to brown lightly. Do not crowd the pot – brown in batches, if necessary. When steak is browned on all sides, remove from pot.

■ Add onions, garlic and mushrooms and stir well. Use a wooden spoon to scratch bottom. Add red wine, stirring until wine reduces by half.

■ Return meat to the pot; add tomato paste, carrots and herbs. Cover with 2 inches of water, add cognac and orange zest and simmer, covered partially, for 1-2 hours, until steak is tender.

■ Remove herb stems and zest pieces from pot. Add orange juice and simmer 15 minutes more.

■ Cook the noodles in boiling salted water for about 8 minutes. Drain and toss with the oil and chopped chives, season with salt. Serve the stew over the noodles and garnish with orange fillets.

HERBS AND GARLIC ROASTED LOIN OF LAMB WITH ROASTED FINGERLING POTATOES

Serves 6

Preheat oven to 450 degrees F.

■ Make a mixture with 1/2 cup olive oil, Dijon and whole sprigs of herbs and garlic. Marinate the lamb for at least one hour. Place lamb in a heavy ovenproof casserole dish that will hold lamb comfortably. Place cut vegetables around base of pan. Season generously salt and pepper. Turn oven down to 400 de F. Bake for 40 minutes, rotating lamb. When finished, an instant thermometer re inserted in the center should register degrees for medium rare.

loin of lamb, approximately 4 pounds
3/4 cup extra virgin olive oil
1/2 cup Dijon mustard
7 large cloves garlic, smashed
2 sprigs thyme
2 sprigs rosemary
cup diced onion
1/2 cup diced celery stalks

1/2 cup diced carrots
1 leek (white part only) washed and sliced to 1/8 inch
1 cup red wine (Merlot or Cabernet)
11/2 pounds fingerling potatoes
1/4 cup olive oil
2 tablespoons fresh rosemary leaves
Salt and pepper

Preparation - Potatoes

Mix potatoes with the rosemary, oil and salt and place in a baking sheet and cover with aluminum foil. Put in the oven for 30 minutes then remove foil and roast for 15 additional minutes until lightly golden and crisp. Remove from the oven and keep warm until ready to be served.

Remove lamb from oven and place in a shallow roasting pan tented with foil, set aside 15 minutes before slicing. Slice 1/2 inch thick, on the bias (3-4 slices per person).

■ Transfer contents of casserole into saucepan. Add the wine to the casserole and scratch the bottom with a wooden spoon (the wine should boil immediately). Bring contents of saucepan to a simmer. Peel remaining garlic and add remainder of herb sprigs. Simmer gently for 30 minutes. Strain, return to saucepan and season with salt and pepper. Serve the lamb over the roasted potatoes and drizzle with the sauce.

BRAISED LAMB CHOPS IN LEMON SAUCE WITH CORN AND GRAIN CAKES

Serves 4

8 lamb chops (not trimmed) at room temperature
1/4 cup olive oil
Salt and pepper
2 garlic cloves, peeled
2 shallots, peeled and chopped
1/4 cup flour
1 egg, beaten
Juice from 1 large lemon
2 cups beef or lamb stock
1/3 cup chopped mint leaves for garnish
1 lemon, quartered

4 1/2 ounces quinoa
3 ounces corn (canned or frozen and thawed)
1 1/2 quarts vegetable stock
1 teaspoon salt
Ground black pepper (as needed)
12 ounces yellow cornmeal
3/4 teaspoon ground cumin
1/2 teaspoon cayenne
4 1/2 ounces cornflake crumbs
1/2 teaspoon vegetable oil

■ Season the chops with salt and pepper, coat in the flour and then in the egg. Heat the oil in a big sauté pan and sauté the chops until golden on both sides. Remove from the pan to a big wide brazing pot that will fit all chops in one layer. In the sauté pan sauté the potatoes, in batches, in the remaining fat for 5 minutes until lightly golden and crisp.

■ Mix the lemon juice with the stock, garlic and shallots and pour over the chops. Season with salt and pepper. Bring to a boil and reduce to low heat. Cook, covered for 1 1/2 hours. Add more liquids if necessary.

Preparation - Cakes:

■ Rinse the quinoa several times in cold water and

■ Cook the quinoa in two cups of the stock, about minutes.
Fluff with a fork and spread on a sheet pan to cool.
Season with 1/4 teaspoon salt and pepper.

■ Bring the remaining 1 quart of stock to a boil. Wh constantly, gradually add 6 ounces of the cornmeal stock. Reduce to a simmer and continue to cook

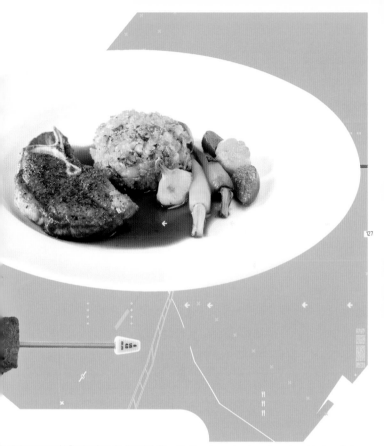

s, stirring constantly. Remove from the heat and stir
orn, quinoa, cumin and cayenne. Season with 1/2
on salt and taste for flavor. Correct seasoning as
. Pour into half sheet pan to cool.

en cool enough to handle, form the mixture into 20
about 2 1/2 ounces each. Refrigerate until needed.

bine the remaining cornmeal with the cornflake
. Heat the oil in a sauté pan; dredge the cakes in
meal mixture and fry for 2 minutes on each side.

■ Place two cakes in each serving plate, lean 2 chops
against the cakes and drizzle with the sauce. Garnish with
the mint leaves and lemon quarters.

HORSERADISH MUSTARD-CRUSTED ROAST BEEF WITH WARM POTATO SALAD AND GRILLED TOMATOES

Serves 6-8

3 pounds eye round roast, cleaned
1 cup grainy horseradish flavored Dijon mustard
2 sprigs rosemary
Butcher twine
3 tablespoons Canola oil
3 pounds bliss potatoes
3 ounces olive oil
2 ounces cider vinegar
2 tablespoons minced shallots
1 1/2 tablespoons Dijon mustard
1 tablespoon chopped parsley
1 1/2 tablespoons chopped tarragon
1 1/2 teaspoons sugar
1/2 teaspoon salt
1/2 teaspoon ground black pepper
2 beefsteak tomatoes
2 tablespoons olive oil
1 teaspoon fresh thyme leaves
Salt and pepper

Preheat oven to 475 degrees F.

Preparation - Salad:

■ Place the potatoes in a pot and cover with water. Bring to a boil and cook until tender. Strain and let cool. When cool enough to handle slice 1/4-inch thick.

■ In a large bowl, whisk together the olive oil, vinegar, shallots and mustard. Add the parsley, tarragon, sugar, salt and pepper. Gently toss the potatoes in the dressing and keep warm.

Season the meat well with salt and pepper and tight oval shape with the butcher twine.

■ Spread the mustard generously all over th and place one sprig of rosemary on eac lengthwise, using the twig to hold it in place.

■ Heat a wide sauté pan or a cast iron skillet minutes. Add the oil and sear the meat on a Remove the meat to a roasting rack and place oven. Roast for 40-45 minutes. The internal temp should be 135 (medium rare). Let stand for 10 r before thinly slicing.

the tomatoes in half, brush each half with the
l and season with salt. Heat a grilling pan and
ery hot grill the tomatoes, skin side down first,
ninutes on each side. Sprinkle with the thyme
while hot. Keep warm until ready to serve.

:e 3-4 tablespoons of the salad in a middle of a
plate. Fan the roast beef slices and add one
nato per plate. The roast beef can be served
·r cold.

Serves 4

For the Kabobs:

2 pounds ground lamb meat
1/2 cup chopped parsley
2 garlic cloves, chopped
1/3 cup chopped onions
1 teaspoon Baharat
(Mediterranean seasoning)
Salt and pepper
3 tablespoons lamb or duck fat

For the Tahini:

1 cup Tahini paste
1/3 cup lemon juice
1/2 cup water
2 garlic cloves
2/3 cup parsley, chopped
1/3 cup cilantro leaves
Salt and pepper
4 ripe but firm tomatoes
2 tablespoons extra virgin olive oil

1/4 cup chopped fresh mint
leaves
1 tablespoon lemon juice
2-3 pita breads
2 tablespoons olive oil
1 garlic clove, halved

at oven to 350 degrees F.

x all the kabob ingredients, but the fat. Make finger-
atties out of the meat and keep in the refrigerator for
a hour.

aration – Tahini:

a food processor, mix the tahini, lemon juice and
Purée for 1 minute. Add the garlic and herbs and
for 20 seconds until herbs are well chopped. Season
th salt and pepper and set aside until ready to serve.

■ Take the green tip off the tomatoes, cut into quarters
and discard the seeds. Dice each quarter and mix with the
olive oil, lemon juice and mint. Season with salt and keep
refrigerated until serving time.

■ Cut the pita bread, horizontally, to create 2 discs. Brush
the discs with the olive oil and rub with the garlic. Cut each
disc into 8 triangles and toast in the oven for 5-7 minutes.

■ Heat the fat in a sauté pan. Fry the kabobs 2 minutes
on each side until brown and crisp but medium in the
middle. Arrange on a plate and drizzle with green tahini.
Serve with pita bread points and chopped tomato salad.

BEEF AND PEAR SKEWERS OVER CRISPY SWEET POTATOES AND GREENS

Serves 4

1 1/2 pounds rib eye, cleaned and diced one-inch thick
3 Bosc pears, washed, seeded and diced one-inch thick
1 medium Vidalia onion or any sweet onion, diced one-inch thick

For the Marinade:
2 shallots, chopped
2 garlic cloves, minced
3 tablespoons good quality pear liquor, apple liqueur or
a good brandy
3 tablespoons grape seed oil
2 tablespoons cider vinegar
1 tablespoon honey
2 tablespoons chopped fresh tarragon leaves
Salt and pepper
3 medium sweet potatoes, washed but not peeled
1/4 cup olive oil
2 tablespoons chopped fresh sage leaves

x all of the marinade ingredients in a bowl. Rub the
dices in the marinade, cover with plastic wrap and
in the fridge for at least 2 hours (up to 24 hours)
the meat every few hours (the marinade should not
the meat completely).

aration – Potatoes:

at oven to 375 degrees F.

ing a mandolin, or a very sharp knife, slice the sweet
es into very thin slices. Gently toss them in the oil
age and season with salt. Arrange them, overlapping,
aking dish and cover with aluminum foil. Bake for 30

minutes. Remove the foil and bake for 20-25 additional
minutes until crispy.

■ Strain the meat from the marinade (keep the marinade
left over) and thread on metal skewers (if using wooden
ones soak them in water for 15 minutes before using)
alternating with pear and onion dices. Brush with the
marinade liquids and season lightly with salt and pepper.

■ Grill over a hot grill, griddle or grilling pan for 3 minutes
on each side. Arrange the sweet potato crisps on a serving
plate, lean 3 skewers on top and top with green salad.

"WHEN YOU INVEST A LOT IN COOKING YOUR
FOOD, THE PRESENTATION SHOULD REFLECT
THAT INVESTMENT."

DESSERTS

CREPE WITH VANILLA PASTRY CREA
AND CITRUS SAUCE
Serves 4-6

he Crepe:	For the Pastry Cream:	For the Sauce:
ces butter	2 cups milk	1 cup fresh squeezed tangerine juice
ces flour	4 ounces sugar	1/2 cup fresh squeezed orange juice
s	3 egg yolks	2 tablespoons lemon juice
ce sugar	1 vanilla bean	3 tablespoons sugar
of salt	1 1/2 ounces cornstarch	1 tablespoon Grand Mariner
cups milk		2 ounces butter, diced small
espoon orange zest		Tangerine segments for garnish
for frying		

aration – Pastry Cream:

ake a slit in the vanilla bean with a small knife,
wise, and scrape some of the vanilla seeds using the
de of the knife. Place the seeds and bean in a
pot with the milk and sugar and heat until sugar
ves (milk should not boil). Beat the yolks in a medium
bowl and mix in the cornstarch. Pour 1/3 of the milk
he yolks and mix well; return the yolk mixture to the
nd whisk constantly over medium low heat for 4
es until it starts to boil and thickens. Transfer to
er dish; cover the exposed cream surface with plastic
and let cool.

aration – Crepes:

elt the butter in a saucepan until lightly golden.
er to a mixing bowl and add the eggs, sugar flour, and
vhile whisking, add the flour and the orange zest

(if lumpy, transfer the batter through a sieve).
Heat a small nonstick pan and butter it lightly. Ladle some
of the crepe batter to the pan swirling the pan to coat
evenly. Fry the crepe 1 minute on each side, remove to a
plate and repeat with the rest of the batter. The crepes
should be as thin as possible.

Preparation – Sauce:

■ Heat a small saucepan for 1 minute over high flame.
Pour the citrus juices to the pan and let simmer. Add the
sugar and stir; pour the liquor and remove from the heat.

■ Spread 3 tablespoons of the pastry cream in the
middle of a crepe, fold in half once, then fold again. Make
2 crepes per serving. Drizzle the sauce on top and around
while hot and garnish with the tangerine segments. Serve
immediately.

ROSE WATER & VANILLA PANNA COTTA WITH STRAWBERRY SAUCE

Serves 6

4 cups heavy cream
1/2 cup sugar
1 vanilla bean or 1 teaspoon vanilla extract
2 tablespoons rose water
2 1/2 teaspoons gelatin powder
2 tablespoons water

For the Sauce

1 cup strawberries, washed and cut in halves
Cheesecloth (optional)
1/3 cup sugar
Rose petals for garnish

■ Mix sugar and cream in a saucepot; split the vanilla bean in half and scrape the seeds into the cream and sugar mixture; throw the vanilla bean in as well. Bring the cream to a boil, mixing well, and reduce heat to a light simmer. Let simmer for 45 minutes.

■ Place gelatin and water in a small saucepan and heat briefly. Stir well until the entire gelatin has dissolved.

■ Strain the cream and add a little of it to the gelatin. Combine both mixtures, then add the rose water and whisk well. Pour into small serving dishes and refrigerate for 4 hours (until set).

■ Blend strawberries and sugar in a food processor to achieve a liquid texture. To get rid of the seeds strain the sauce through the cheesecloth.

■ Remove the panna cotta from the mold and transfer to a plate. Pour around with sauce, garnish with fresh strawberries and the rose petals. Serve.

GRILLED BANANAS AND MASCARPONE CREAM NAPOLEON WITH PINEAPPLE SAUCE

Serves 4

For the Twills:
1 pound brown sugar
13 ounces butter
1 pound dark corn syrup
2 1/2 cups all purpose flour
13 ounces almonds, finely chopped

For the Mascarpone C
1 pound Mascarpone ch
1/3 cup rum
1/3 cup sugar
4 firm bananas
1/3 cup brown sugar
2 ounces melted butter
2 cups unsweetened cru
pineapple
1 tablespoon sugar
1 tablespoon lime juice
1/4 cup pina colada (or
colada mix)

heat oven to 350 degrees F.

Bring the sugar, corn syrup and butter to a boil in rge saucepot. Let boil over medium low heat for inutes. Remove from the heat.

Mix the flour and the almonds with the syrup, n transfer to a bowl and let cool completely.

Line a baking sheet with parchment paper or a pad. With wet hands make small balls out of the er and flatten them on the baking pan leaving ugh space between each one. Bake for 15 utes. Transfer from the pan, while still warm, to a surface.

Mix the sugar, mascarpone cheese and rum ether with a whisk.

■ Slice the bananas on the bias (1/8-inch thick). Brush with the butter and sprinkle with sugar. Heat a grilling pan and when very hot, grill the bananas for 1 minute on each side.

■ Heat the crushed pineapple and sugar in a saucepan and add the lime juice. Remove from the heat and mix in the pina colada.

■ Place one twill cookie on a plate, along with 2 tablespoons of the mascarpone cream. Spread 3-4 grilled banana slices and top with another cookie. Gently repeat with another layer. A cookie should be placed on top.

■ Drizzle around with sauce and garnish with edible flowers.

ART REFERENCES

DESSERTS

ACKNOWLEDGEMENTS

Special thanks to my wife Molly Ben for letting me stay up so late every
night. Thanks to Oren Moshe, Yana Kuzin-Ilan, Yossi Melamed, Marilyn
Jefferson, Ellen Linde, Michael Linde, Lisa Marie Meller, The Orchard,
Yoseph Friedman, Nir Dubnikov, Jack & Annet Benishai, Yael & Assaf
Benishai, Sarit & benny Kimchy, Shane Vardi, Shoshana Kirchenboum,
Marketability, Book Tools, Refael Ashkenazi, Motty Benishai, Avi Glatt,
Petal Pride, Yakov Bertwain, Ronit & Rami Soosi, Zohar Vilboosh, Zila
Paletz, Ruby Gelman, Sammy Ayal, Kaufman & Zilberberg, Abrahham
Holzberg and to my dear son David Jonathan and his friends. Deep
appreciation to Ross Exley.